# MATCH MENTALITY

# MATCH MENTALITY
## Becoming a Competitive Shooter

# BEN STOEGER WITH JOEL PARK

Foreword by Tyler Turner

Skyhorse Publishing

Skyhorse Publishing books may be purchased in bulk at special
discounts for sales promotion, corporate gifts, fund-raising, or
educational purposes. Special editions can also be created to
specifications. For details, contact the Special Sales Department,
Skyhorse Publishing, 307 West 36th Street, 11th Floor, New York, NY
10018 or info@skyhorsepublishing.com.

Skyhorse® and Skyhorse Publishing® are registered trademarks of
Skyhorse Publishing, Inc.®, a Delaware corporation.

Visit our website at www.skyhorsepublishing.com.

Please follow our publisher Tony Lyons on Instagram
@tonylyonsisuncertain

10 9 8 7 6 5 4 3 2 1

Library of Congress Cataloging-in-Publication Data is available on file.

Print ISBN: 978-1-5107-7941-9
eBook ISBN: 978-1-5107-7942-6

Cover design by David Ter-Avanesyan
Printed in China

# Contents

# FOREWORD: THE MENTAL GAME

Practical shooters hear a lot of talk about the mental game. It's a frequent topic of discussion on podcasts, on the internet, and on the Range. Everyone understands on an intuitive level that a superior mental game will improve one's shooting. But in my experience, few shooters bother to examine the mental game beyond a very shallow and superficial level.

This leads to some predictable results. In some camps, the mental game has an aura of mysticism or quasi-spirituality around it. (I find it kind of surreal to overhear Zen Buddhist concepts debated on a gun range.) Some think mental game is a secret cheat code, that once discovered and applied, is the key to unlocking the shooting god within, waiting only to be released. For many, mental game is a convenient scapegoat to be blamed for mistakes, ineffective training, and underwhelming match results. Still others think of mental game as reducible to a mathematical formula for success—that following a particular series of carefully calculated steps will equal the desired result.

Maybe there is some truth in those conceptualizations of the mental game. However, I don't think any one of them in isolation does a complete job. Here's my analogy: The mental game is like the operating system of a computer. It's always running. It's always facilitating communication between software and hardware, processing and memorizing data, and making stuff happen. We never think strictly about the OS when we're using the computer. We think about a particular app we're using to edit video, or the game we're playing, or the message we're writing in a word processor; but none of that would happen without an OS. Likewise, it's a big problem if your OS is not equipped to handle the various applications and functions we wish to run. If you've ever had a computer crash or bricked a phone, you know what I mean. The same holds true if we feed the OS junk information or fail to update the security patch and get a virus.

Consider this: The mental game is the OS through which we apply everything we know and do in practical shooting. Everything is tied into and runs through this mental matrix, including our technical skills and abilities, our learning style and practice methodologies, our memories, our emotions, our decisions, our motor skills, and our judgments. You can't stop it and you can't "solve" it. Everything in life affects it. But you can manage it, and you can use it to your benefit.

This book is a manual for you to learn to do just that: Manage the mental game and use it to your benefit. Ben and Joel have purposely created this book to be a practical and actionable guide to developing your own mental skills. Consider the incredible depth of experience from which these lessons come. I sincerely hope you'll apply these concepts and upgrade your own "operating system."

*Tyler Turner - USPSA Production Grand Master*

# PART 1
# INTRODUCTION

# CHAPTER 1

# IT'S MORE THAN JUST SHOOTING

Imagine some targets, a bunch of USPSA targets. Most of them are inside ten yards. There are a few poppers, a single moving target (a drop turner, nothing complicated), and a few no-shoots scattered around. None of the shots are all that challenging. For a serious shooter who has been training for years, there is absolutely nothing complicated about the stage I am describing, nothing at all.

If you take the same target scenario and add into the mix that this is at USPSA Nationals, then the situation becomes a lot more challenging. If you have attended a USPSA Nationals or a European Handgun Championship or even a World Shoot, you know that these high-level matches are somehow different. The amount of pressure that people are under to do well is immense and often overwhelming. It doesn't matter that the demand to do well is self-imposed, and the goals they are trying to achieve are their own. What is very real is that you can feel a very different atmosphere in the big matches. It's in the air.

Now, imagine you are winning a match like that. All you need to do is shoot one more stage. The targets are the same ones described above. Your lead is such that as long as you shoot this stage without falling on your face, you are going to be National Champion. Even though the targets are nothing special, the situation is very special. This scenario is a once in a lifetime for many people. Your hands are shaking, and your heart is beating out of your chest. "Just shoot the stage without doing anything stupid!" you think to yourself. Can you do it?

This book isn't about shooting as much as it is about the preparation, complicated feelings, emotions, and physiological changes that will occur when you are in a competition. I have been that guy praying not to screw up a Nationals and I know what that feels like. Your technical training and talent can take you very far in the shooting sports, and it will allow you the opportunity to win matches that matter to you. Your mental fortitude, visualization, and competition mindset are factors that will enable you to carry through and actually win.

The simple fact is that practical shooting matches test more than your technical shooting ability. They assess the professionalism of your preparation. Did you check and test your gear? Did you ensure that you didn't leave anything to chance that you could possibly control?

At face value, matches test your ability to develop a stage plan, memorize it, and execute it. When things go wrong (not if), it is up to you and you alone to minimize the damage and get back on your plan.

On a deeper level, matches test your ability to deal with pressure and control yourself. If people got mulligans for their bad runs and do-overs for train wreck stages, we would have an entirely different definition of top winners at our sport. These top winners would be rewarded for their best repeated attempts. Our sport rewards you for being able to deliver your peak performance on the initial and only attempt at a stage run and will "punish" harshly for poor runs and train wreck stages. The fact that you own your mistakes and poor runs has a dramatic impact on risk management with your shooting. Managing all of this in your mind while shooting a stage is not easy.

Honing these skills, these "mental game" sorts of things, are what this book is all about.

# CHAPTER 2
# WHY ARE YOU HERE?

Before you start on a journey toward Practical Shooting excellence, you should think carefully about what it is you want to get out of this journey. It is unlikely you are reading this book without ever having shot a USPSA or IPSC match. You have probably done some training and are looking to improve. You may perhaps want to skip ahead in the book and get to the "good stuff" about how to shoot better scores in matches. I strongly encourage you to carefully consider what it is you are trying to accomplish and get yourself on a plan directed toward that goal.

For many people, participating in practical shooting matches is the primary thing they spend their free time and money on. It is a hobby that does not always lend itself to casual participation. I have seen many people turn this sport into an obsession that has taken over their life. I would certainly count myself among these people.

What you need to think about is what it is you really want to get out of competitive shooting. This is important to understand so you can align your efforts with your expectations and set goals that make sense to you. Setting expectations too high and putting in a low level of effort will lead to frustration and can kill your enjoyment of the sport. It also doesn't make much sense to set the bar too low and then shoot fifty thousand rounds a year to accomplish nothing in particular. Honestly assessing where you are, where you want to go, and what it will take to get there is very important for long-term, sustained participation in the sport, as well as your own mental stability.

So, ask yourself. . . . Why are you here?

Do you want a hobby that gives you something to do when you aren't working and have a bit of free time?

Do you want a social activity to participate in with friends for fun and camaraderie?

Do you want an excuse to travel around to different regions or different countries and use the sport as a reason to see places you would never otherwise go to?

Maybe you like the idea of having a sport that you can train for a little bit every day to keep active and have something fun to do.

You might just like guns and like the idea of attending matches and shooting different guns.

Of course, there is no "correct" answer for any of this. People have different goals and different motivations for participating in the sport, and that is absolutely fine. What will cause problems is if you do not ask yourself why you are doing any of this or acknowledge what it is you are hoping to accomplish in your shooting career.

To illustrate why this is important, consider a common scenario with a new shooter. Imagine a talented young newcomer who is physically fit, smart, etc. This person gets to Master class in USPSA within two years of shooting his first match and is a solid shooter at his local club. He always wins his division at every match unless there is some sort of catastrophic equipment or other issue. He might even win a state section match in his second year of USPSA.

This shooter obviously has potential. This person's friends talk about how well he is doing. Everyone is impressed with him, etc. This person then sets the goal of winning USPSA Nationals in his third year of shooting. He runs up some credit card debt purchasing ammunition and guns for training. He climbs from fifteen thousand rounds of training ammo in year two to an eighty thousand-round year in his third year. This puts stress on his significant other because of all the time and money he has invested in competition shooting. This shooter finishes at 72 percent at USPSA Nationals. The first day was a disaster due to match pressure at a level he had never experienced previously. Although days two and three were a bit better, this person never really had a chance to win the match.

This shooter then backs off on his practice schedule quite a lot in the fourth year of participation. After all . . . what was the point? He shot a lot for a year and still didn't achieve his goal or anything close to it. At the end of year four, his competitive career has kind of run its course. He burned out in the third year and never really got the drive back. He shoots two or three club matches in year five and then never attends a USPSA match again.

The above story is a common one. It is something I have seen happen many times in my shooting career. What really happened is someone with a lot of talent and motivation came into the sport, and then their expectations became incompatible with reality. They set themselves up for burnout and failed expectations and then exited USPSA. This whole situation could have been avoided if, at the beginning, they carefully considered their goals, and moderated their effort expended in USPSA/shooting sports. Instead of putting in a ton of money, time, and energy into USPSA for a year, and in their own mind feeling that they got nothing out of it, they could have more gradually ramped up their training and participation with realistic goals.

The above example is one of many ways that improper goal setting leads to dissatisfaction in the shooting sports. Many similar situations can occur, and that is just one example. Let me describe a few common scenarios where the input is properly balanced with the output.

## Casual Participation

If your only goal is to shoot and have a good time, you are a casual participant. This will not require a whole lot of training effort. Let's say you just want to train when it is convenient for you, and you have a friend to train with. Your primary purpose for training is to be familiar with your gear and make sure your gun hits where you point it. To you, training is really just more of an opportunity to shoot and have fun, not really directed toward any concrete goals. You enjoy going to the range to train, but if you didn't feel like going that day, you wouldn't go. You might do a little dry training, or you might not, if it's not fun or interesting you generally don't do it.

Your level of ability is going to settle wherever your age, physical condition, and aptitude for the sport puts you. For a young shooter who learns quickly, is in good shape, and is smart, that may well mean Master class. For someone on the other side of the age or talent curve, it might be D class. It just depends on each person's unique situation. What I wouldn't expect to happen is to have that situation change a whole lot over time. Even a talented young shooter isn't going to realize their full potential without putting in sustained effort over time.

Casual participation is fine, as long as you are happy with where your "natural" talent level puts you in the sport. It essentially means you show up for matches and practice a little bit if and when you feel like it. If you start shooting and get into B class without a whole lot of effort and you are happy with that level, then that's great. You may even occasionally win a club match depending on what the normal talent pool is, and who else decides to show up that day.

What you should not expect when engaging in casual participation is to see significant and steady progress over time, especially once you've reached mid-level in the sport. Improvement beyond that comes from training consistently, even when you don't feel like it. Shooting casually a little bit now and then when you feel like it isn't really training at the level required to climb to the upper levels of the sport.

## Serious Participation

Serious participation includes putting in sustained training effort over time. People who are doing regular training, especially more than once a week, are participating at a serious level. Daily dry practice and weekly live training, or some other similar schedule are common with a serious participation level. Serious participants often read books about shooting and search for tips in online forums.

They might review match footage of themselves and other shooters and analyze it.

People at this level of participation likely have their ego tied up in their match results. They tend to get nervous on classifier stages or at big matches. They put in regular sustained effort and have a sincere desire to get better.

Results are not guaranteed by participating at this level, but your odds of improving steadily over time are much higher. A good plan for improvement is still required in order to get results, but the level of effort is the important part we are trying to define here. Serious participants put in effort beyond what a casual shooter does.

In order to win big matches, most people at the very least will be at this serious level of participation. More often than not, a person who attains Grand Master classification was at least engaging in a serious participation level for some length of time to get there.

## High-Level Participation

Shooters at a high level of participation are training daily. They get to the range once or twice a week and more than likely dry fire daily. They understand the requirements necessary to compete at a high level, are willing to put in the effort, and possess a high level of dedication to the sport. They plan their schedule around matches and prioritize training time in their daily lives. They think about shooting constantly and are always planning the next steps in their training.

These are the shooters consistently winning section matches and possibly area matches depending on who else shows up. They have an emotional connection to shooting and analyze every match they shoot. They may even track others in the sport and check match results for events they themselves didn't even attend. These shooters are motivated to continually improve their performance and it is a primary focus for them.

## Pro Level Participation

Professional level participation is for those who are industry professionals or want to be industry professionals in some capacity. These are competitors who are sponsored at the level where they draw compensation from some industry-related company and have their careers on the line at some level when they attend matches. If they want to be a top instructor, they need to produce top results at competitions in order to draw clients. People who want to earn a living in the sport, or have a chance of winning against those who do, need to treat their shooting the same way as the Professionals do.

This means that training is their top priority and a regular part of their life. Thousands of dollars are going to be spent on ammunition and training equipment (assuming nobody is giving them that stuff). Top industry people may shoot in excess of 100k rounds a year. If they shoot less than that, more than likely they are doing high amounts of dry-fire training.

A Professional will spare no expense when it comes to equipment. Pros will not hesitate to acquire the guns they prefer or the right ammunition. Gear is extensively tested before it makes a debut and used in a match. Generally speaking, Professionals take almost any match as seriously as they would take a USPSA Nationals match. Pros have so much self-image wrapped up in their shooting performance that they may have their mood destroyed by a poor showing. For most Pros, a USPSA National title is something they will hang their hat on for the rest of their lives. To reiterate, even if you aren't a sponsored Professional shooter, you must train like a pro if you have any hope of winning against them.

| MAIN GOAL | |
| --- | --- |
| I WANT TO: | QUANTIFY IT: |
| Make A class in USPSA | One year from now (May 1, 2024) |

| WHERE I AM CURRENTLY: | |
| --- | --- |
| MY STARTING POINT IS: | MY GOAL IS REALISTIC FROM HERE: |
| C class (46.67%) in USPSA | YES |

| SUB-GOALS NEEDED TO REACH MAIN GOAL: | |
| --- | --- |
| I NEED TO: | QUANTIFY IT: |
| Dry Fire | 4 times/week for 30 mins. each |
| Live Fire Practice | Every other week |
| Shoot Classifiers in a match | Twice a month |

| I WILL REEVALUATE THIS GOAL: |
| --- |
| Six months from now |

*Figure 1: Setting realistic goals that are measurable are key to your development as a shooter. You should be able to break your main goal into sub-goals that are quantifiable to assist you in getting to where you want to be. Use this example to set and achieve your own goals; blank charts have been included in the back of the book for your use.*

# CHAPTER 3

# DEFINING YOUR PATH IN THE SPORT

It is likely obvious to you what level of participation makes sense for your situation and mindset, given what you are willing to put in and what you want to get out of the sport. Your participation level may change over time, and that's fine. You might start out as a casual shooter who shoots once a month, then training once a month turns into training every other weekend, and before you know it, you're practicing every weekend. I've also seen lots of new competitors shoot a few matches and enjoy it so much they dive in headfirst and start training hard right away because they are having so much fun learning their new sport.

Life events can also affect your level of participation and priorities. Maybe you just got a new job that is taking up more of your time, or perhaps you just had a baby. You might not be able to stay on your current training schedule until things quiet down, and then you may ramp up your training again. It's essential to manage your expectations during life event changes and adjust your plan accordingly.

One crucial thing to point out is that there are inherent limitations to what you are going to be able to accomplish in practical shooting given your age, motivation, physical condition, finances, and whatever other constraints you might care to add to that list. An overweight fifty-year-old that has never fired a gun before is starting in a very different place than a fourteen-year-old with wealthy parents who also happens to shoot. If you found your way to this book, you probably don't need specific facts of life explained to you, but it never hurts to have a reality check. The oldest shooter I am aware of who made it to the upper echelon of the sport started in his late thirties. Most top shooters began in their twenties at the latest.

The financial strains associated with shooting are very real. If you don't have excess financial means, you can still rise up in the sport, but you will find yourself constrained with two very real aspects of your shooting budget. One will be financial; planning for expenses related to travel and associated costs with major matches. The other will be budgeting your use of ammunition carefully; split between using it for training and for matches. Plenty of people have accomplished a lot in the sport without spending a lot of money, and it can be done, just not easily.

Once you settle on where you see yourself in the big picture of the sport, then you should start thinking about setting some intermediate goals. For example, you might have a goal of winning the USPSA Nationals. Right now, that goal is more like a dream. Maybe you are classified as C and have never attended a Nationals. At this point, you are so far away from your dream it is really counterproductive to focus on the end goal. You need some smaller milestones to reach first.

What you should do is reverse engineer your dream and start planning an actual path to get there.

USPSA National Champions are generally going to win any state-level matches that they attend. They are going to rank very high at any Area match. They are classified as GMs. They can draw their gun in X time at X range (you can spend some time on YouTube watching those guys do what they do). You can travel as far down this rabbit hole as you want to, because by working the problem in reverse it is going to show you how to move forward.

As far away from winning Nationals as you are sitting in C class and having never been to Nationals, you can figure out a starting goal that IS reachable for you. Do you imagine that a National Champion can shoot 10 shots in a row in the A zone of a target at 25 yards with no time limit? I think they can. If you haven't figured out how to do that, then that is a logical goal that isn't a dream. You have a gun, you practice at a shooting range, all you need to do is figure out how to get the gun to hit where you point it without a time limit. By working your way backward from where you want to go, you now have a first step toward your dream.

Realistically, a National Championship is more of a delusion than a goal for most people. That's just the way it is. However, there are always ways you can move forward in your game. You can move up in classification level. You can win your state match. You can aim for Top 16 or Top 10 at Nationals. You can develop amazing gun handling skills that almost look like some sort of trick to the untrained eye. There is always a next step, and you need to decide for yourself what that next step is.

Your goals shouldn't be rigidly fixed; you should be reviewing them periodically and adjusting when necessary (Figure 2). This is more of an ongoing thought process than something you are bound to forever. For example, if you have a goal of making master in open division, but later on down the line you decide to change divisions, you obviously should discard that original goal and pick a goal that makes sense for your new division.

It is important to understand that some goals are things that are entirely within your complete control, and some are merely subject to your influence. If your goal is to beat a particular person at a specific match . . . well, that is something you have some influence over, but you don't have complete control. That other person could step up their training or leverage some strategy that you haven't thought of, and your goal will become effectively impossible to accomplish. Similarly, they could fall on their face at the match, and your goal will essentially accomplish itself. You should understand what the possible outcomes are when you set a goal, and keep your expectations in check.

The obvious goal that most people tend to gravitate toward is that of winning particular trophies. Although winning your class or division at matches is great, it isn't the most productive goal for maintaining your perspective and motivation over the long term. Let me explain why this is.

If you want to win a specific match (let's say your state section match in your favorite division) and you think this is a realistic goal for yourself, then you may decide to set that as your training goal. Let's say you shot 92 percent of the division winner last year. You decide you want to train up and win this year, so you need to improve 8 percent over last year. On the surface, this seems like a good idea, you have a goal.

The reality is that lots of things can happen at a match. Maybe your main rival switches to a different division at your goal match. Let's say a pro-level shooter shows up and shoots your division. Perhaps your rival competitor goes nuts training and takes four classes over the course of the year and shoots 80k training rounds. The list of potential scenarios that could derail your goal is almost limitless. These scenarios may result in you completing your goal or not, and it may well not have much to do with anything that you did or did not do in your training, it was luck of the draw.

If you don't maintain a proper perspective, you may lose motivation very quickly or maybe set yourself up for losing your motivation down the road. Let me give you an example. You step up your training for six months prior to your goal match. You shoot 30k rounds and do daily dry-fire training. This represents a doubling of your investment in terms of time and training ammo. You finish at 94 percent at the match, only a 2 percent change from the year before. If you fail to take into account the fact that your rival did three times the training that you did, you may lose a lot of motivation to train. Doubling your effort for only a 2 percent change? That doesn't pass the cost-benefit analysis test for most people.

Consider a nearly opposite scenario: Perhaps your rival changes divisions and you get the win you were seeking almost automatically without changing the amount of effort you are putting in. If you start to get an inflated sense of your own ability or skills, then you are setting yourself up for a big disappointment down the road as well.

A much cleaner way to measure your progress is to set goals for your own individual skills and performance, without regard to anyone else. Are you able to shoot a clean match? Are you improving your draw time? Can you shoot X drill in Y time with Z hits? These sorts of things are much simpler to measure, they are completely within your control, and they should keep your ego in line with reality. This is a much more realistic and productive way to set goals and measure your progress toward them. Of course, if you stay focused in this manner on improving your technical and competition skills, you are going to win plenty of trophies as a byproduct. But this success in matches will be a result of achieving the individual skill and performance goals you set for yourself, not the goal in itself.

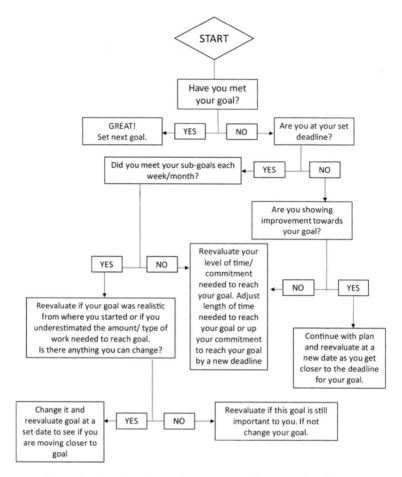

*Figure 2: You should reevaluate your goal at a set deadline to ensure you are on track. The above flow chart will assist you to ensure you are being honest with yourself in achieving your goals. This should also include checking on your sub-goals.*

# PART 2
# MATCH MENTALITY

# CHAPTER 4
# GAINING MATCH MENTALITY

From Joel:

I was at my first big match of the year after a Spring of heavy training. I slept fairly well the night before the match, but I was nervous and excited. My skills were the strongest they had ever been, and I felt ready for my first showdown with a rival I had never beat before. I felt calm when I woke up, but started to get really nervous as I got to the range and was putting my gear on. I went to the safe area to dry fire before the match started so I could calm down. It didn't help. I couldn't even get my draws quite right. I tried to calm down, but nothing was working. I was visibly shaking and hoped no one would notice.

I was squadded with my rival and watched him shoot the first stage. He shot the stage well, but I knew I could go faster. I had the chance to pull ahead of him on the first stage. All I had to do was push a little bit, and I'd have the lead right out of the gate. A few friends noticed how nervous I was and made comments trying to help me calm down. I decided the only thing I could do was hope my skills would carry me through.

I shot the stage with two misses, one penalty, and a fast time. I completely fell apart at the start signal and sprayed bullets at the targets. I had lost the match on the first stage. I absolutely crumbled under pressure, and it was the pressure I brought with me.

The rest of the match went well with several stage wins after the pressure was off, and I was "competing for second place" in my mind. It blew my mind how much better I was shooting when the pressure was off, and I didn't think I could come close to winning. Looking back, I was way too quick to give up over one bad stage. I just assumed everyone else would have a perfect match, and my match had to be perfect to win.

I can still remember the feelings I had during the match and on the drive home. I decided if I ever wanted to win anything, I would need to learn how to deal with pressure. This match was a significant turning point in my shooting career.

*Joel Park, USPSA Production Grand Master*

While Practical Shooting competition is an excellent test of your equipment and shooting ability, there is undoubtedly another significant factor in play; your skills are going to be tested under very real pressure. In my opinion, the shooters who win championships regularly are the ones who can hold together under the crushing pressure at big matches like USPSA Nationals or an IPSC World Shoot.

# CHAPTER 5
# WHAT IS
# MATCH PRESSURE?

When we talk about match pressure, we are referring to the state of anxiety that exists during matches in the minds and bodies of competitors. Sweating, increased heart rate, loss of sleep, and persistent worry are just a few of the things that match pressure can produce.

Discussing pressure at matches isn't a common topic to address. It isn't considered "macho" to talk about pressure. Most shooters feel this immense pressure at certain times during a match, and most internalize it and never really understand what is going on or how to control it. It's a good idea to do a little bit of analysis of your own feelings about competing and get a handle on what you need to do to keep match pressure under control.

## You Bring It with You

The first thing to understand about match pressure is that you bring it with you to the match. It is a reflection of your own thoughts, feelings, desires, and beliefs. That might sound silly, but it is true. You probably desire to do well at the match, maybe you genuinely want a championship or to beat a specific person. Perhaps you believe another shooter is faster or better than you, and you feel intimidated watching them shoot. Maybe you feel very confident at one-handed shooting, and you know the weak-handed stage should go well for you.

The list of examples of how match pressure can appear is endless. The core thing to understand is that match pressure is about you. You bring it with you to a match. It is about your own thoughts and emotions. It is not about anyone else, and nobody else can directly force you to do anything one way or the other in terms of creating or alleviating your pressure.

### Your Level of Involvement

As you invest more time and energy into the sport, you will naturally raise your level of expectations for your performance. You will gain technical skills from practicing and will want to see those abilities pay off in a match. As your capabilities continue to increase, you will expect your match performance to increase as well.

You might put pressure on yourself to beat someone because you feel you train harder than they do. Imagine training for a match and squadding with someone who you consider your match nemesis. While chatting before the match, they tell you that they've been busy with work and haven't been able to practice in weeks. You are currently training daily and feel really prepared. After hearing about your rival's lack of training, don't you deserve to win more than they do since you prepared more? Imagine the feeling you would have if they beat you without putting in the same level of effort you did. That feeling adds pressure on you to perform well, you don't want to feel bad about yourself if you lose to someone who doesn't practice.

Pressure can also come indirectly from your peers. Your friends see you getting better, and they expect to see you do well. Of course, you don't want to look like a fool in front of them, and you don't want to have your friends ask you why you had a miss or slow time.

Your perception of time and the impact of mistakes will likely be very poor when you're under match pressure. For example, waiting for a second pass on a moving target, or watching a popper fall during an activation sequence might feel like an eternity while you are looking through the sights. However, when you watch it on video later you realize it wasn't nearly as bad as you thought. Another example would be shooting a stage while you are relaxed and under control, and everything seems very slow. Watching it on the video may tell an entirely different story, showing you were actually shooting very fast. You might feel fast or slow during a stage, but those are not feelings you can always trust. Match pressure definitely affects your perception while shooting.

## Expectations of Other People

After you have won a few big matches, people start to have big expectations of you. There is nothing that illustrates this quite so much as shooting the season after winning a USPSA National title.

In the highly competitive world of USPSA, pretty much anything can happen, and matches are often decided by just a few match points. One mistake or issue can cause you to fall back three places in the match ranking. The margins are just so tight. However, after you have won Nationals, people expect you to win any match you go to, no matter how much you have been training or who you are shooting against.

You may find yourself in a situation where you feel like a slave to other people's expectations of you. It isn't an enjoyable place to be. I have personally made a point to try to ignore what people say about me, even if it is positive. I want to be shooting for myself for my own reasons and not for other people or to satisfy their expectations. Ignoring the peanut gallery, no matter if the feedback is positive or negative, has proven to be the best way for me to go.

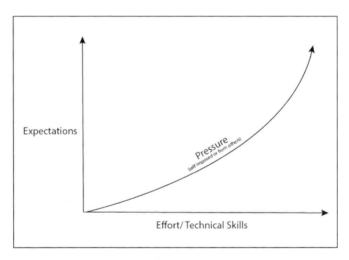

*Figure 3: As a shooter's effort and technical skill increases, the expectations for that shooter also grow. This increases the pressure on that shooter, either self-imposed or via others.*

## Pressure Never Goes Away

Many wish there was some trick, tool or suggestion to make all the pressure go away. Unfortunately, there isn't. No matter how many major matches you enter, you will still feel the same pressure time and time again. Since it's not going away, the key is learning how to manage the pressure you feel and not allowing it to derail your match or compromise your performance. This is much easier said than done, of course.

## Pressure Affects Everyone Differently

If you have shot a lot of matches, you have probably seen everything from someone visibly shaking because they are so nervous, to someone in a close race for the win who looks completely calm like they don't have a care in the world. More than likely, both of those people are equally nervous, they just might not be outwardly showing it.

## Positive Effects of Pressure

Match pressure isn't entirely a negative force, it has positive effects as well. Many people experience a very sharp focus on the task or problem at hand when under pressure. As long as it doesn't escalate to hypervigilance or some other sort of nervous reaction, it is often a net positive.

You might also find that during moments of high pressure, you will feel stronger and not tire as easily. Your body does an excellent job of releasing chemicals to help you use your "gross" muscle functions. Some people find they need to "amp" themselves up because adding pressure will boost their performance, and their performance will be better than if they were totally relaxed.

# CHAPTER 6

# WAYS TO MITIGATE PRESSURE

Since we know the pressure won't ever go away, how should you learn to manage it? One of the most helpful methods is putting yourself in high pressure situations over and over again to build experience dealing with it. Imagine organizing a class or small practice group and the feeling you would have when you need to demonstrate a drill with ten people standing there watching. You don't want to have a bad draw, you don't want to have trigger freeze, and you definitely don't want to miss the target. What will everyone think if you can't even demonstrate the drill correctly? Will they think you don't know what you're talking about? Imagine being in that position. You've executed this drill hundreds of times on your own, what if you make a mistake when everyone is watching? How would you deal with that pressure? This is a great simulation of match pressure, and learning to overcome it will be very helpful for you.

Watching video of a stage where you felt a lot of pressure can be very beneficial. Think of a stage where you were particularly nervous and feeling a lot of pressure. Maybe it was the last stage of a match, and it was the first time you could actually win your division. Perhaps you were only a few percent away from a higher classification, and a classifier stage you shot was the deciding factor if you would earn the higher classification. Watching videos of those kinds of situations before you train can help heighten your sense of pressure. Remember the feelings you had, remember how nervous you were, recreate that feeling in practice so you can learn to mitigate it. Putting yourself in situations like that in practice will only make you better. Everyone handles pressure differently, and training in high-pressure situations is about the only way to learn to work through it since everyone processes things differently.

Math is a tool you can use in training to help you feel more comfortable and confident in matches by tracking hit factor on drills. After you feel warmed up during practice, set up a drill. Shoot it several times while really pushing and try to achieve the highest hit factor you possibly can. Write down each score separately by time and hits, and calculate the hit factor. Then reshoot the same drill and shoot it comfortably. Don't try to achieve a personal best, just shoot the targets, and record the scores for each run the way you did previously. Compare the results of the two groups and see which group was more successful as a whole if it was at a match. Unless you get lucky and really hook up that day, the drills you shoot comfortably will often yield a higher combined total.

After drawing that conclusion, it should take some of the pressure off knowing that you don't need to accomplish a personal best on every stage to get your best match score. All you have to do at the match is shoot the targets comfortably in the way you already know how to. Why would you want to push hard on every stage knowing that you're likely going to score lower than if you shot comfortably? You wouldn't. The knowledge you gain from training with hit factor can give you the confidence to make the right decisions on how you shoot the match.

**Confidence**

Another thing that can help is gaining confidence from training on various shooting challenges in practice sessions and recalling that experience during a match. It's very comforting when you walk onto a stage and know you can make every shot since you've made the same shots in practice over and over. You can also relate target arrays in a match to drills you have shot, remembering how those targets need to be shot for the best result, and recalling yourself successfully doing it in practice. Think of the fundamental skills you've practiced as Lego bricks—you look at a stage and recognize which pieces need to be snapped together to build what you need for a successful stage result. Imagine seeing a fifteen-yard headbox target in a match. Everyone is talking about how tight that shot is, then you think back to shooting a "Distance Change-Up" drill. The goal of "distance change up" is learning to shoot a close target fast, then slowing down to shoot accurately on distant targets. The standard setup for that drill is the far target being a fifteen-yard head box target. Remembering your success in practice, and using that experience to boost your confidence can allow you to be very comfortable on a target that others might be nervous about.

The key is finding things to add to your confidence, which will go a long way toward mitigating pressure. Your personal experience might be completely different from how other people perceive things, or even what is being described here. Maybe shooting "comfortably" will not give you the best result. It could feel like "damage control" or cause you to shoot too slowly if your tendency is to shoot more conservatively. Shooting with a bit of aggression might give you the kick you need to move from "just don't lose," to "I am going to win." Doing the math and paying attention to your confidence level during your training is the key to figuring out the best mindset for you.

### Warming Up into the Match

One of the most common issues that people bring up is the "first stage jitters" or some other variation on the idea that they do worse on their first stage or first few stages than the other stages. First of all, this is an entirely normal feeling, pretty much everyone feels better and more confident after they "warm up." Perhaps a more precise way of putting it is that people tend to do better after they burn off a bit of stress, nerves or jitters on the first stage. The issue isn't so much that you need to shoot some rounds to "warm-up," it's not the actual shooting that lowers the stress level, it's the experience of engaging in the match. The level of nervousness dissipates after a while in the match naturally, often allowing you to shoot at your best later in the match. Ideally you should already be "warmed up" from dry training on the day of the match, using this as a tool to lower your stress level on the first stage.

Pay close attention to what comes out of your mouth at a match, as what you say can directly affect your mindset. Think about someone who makes excuses before they shoot a stage: "Well, I'm not sure how this is going to go," "Let's just see what happens," "I've been too busy to practice," etc. These kinds of statements indicate a lack of readiness for the job, and specifically a lack of confidence. If you are indicating uncertainty or lack of readiness in things you say to other people, then you probably need to do a better job with your preparation next time. What you say and how you talk about your shooting matters a lot.

The best solution for the first stage jitters is to monitor your feelings and emotions carefully and ensure you have a positive focus. Confidence you have gained from your training should make this easier over time. Also, you probably should not start pushing hard for your maximum performance in the early stages of the match since most people are more likely to make mistakes at this point. Be smart and play the long game, you will be better off for it.

# CHAPTER 7

# INTIMIDATION

Even the best shooters occasionally feel intimidated by the skills of others. There is no point naming names, but you can probably think of a top shooter who reloads like greased lightning or one who can run a plate rack as fast as he can pull the trigger. No matter what skillset you think about, there is someone who is insanely good at it. Watching someone do something that they are incredible at can be intimidating if you don't feel like you have, or can ever have, that level of skill.

What you do with that intimidation is up to you. Seeing top shooters do incredible things on Instagram or YouTube can be a serious fuel for your training fire if you take it as an inspiration. That feeling of inadequacy that you likely have when comparing yourself to a top shooter can be turned around to your advantage as motivation while you build new skills.

At a match, however, intimidation can pressure you into making mistakes. Trying to gain an advantage early, or trying to push hard to win the match on the first stage would be a common result of feeling intimidated by the competition. This often results in unforced errors and the exact opposite result from what you were trying to achieve.

The solution for intimidation is to focus on your own skills and the things you are confident you can do. Maybe you have a super slick and consistent draw. Perhaps you are incredibly accurate. Whatever it is, you have strong points too, and you need to leverage those to the maximum advantage. It's ok to acknowledge the strengths of other shooters, just don't forget about your own strengths, and definitely don't think you need to duplicate what someone else can do in order to be successful. There is no perfect competitor, all have individual strengths and weaknesses. The most successful are those with the most strengths and those who use their strengths to the maximum advantage, while minimizing their weaknesses.

From Joel:

It was a hot summer day, and I was squadded with some of my closest friends at a section match in another state. I was nervous during the first few stages, and I calmed down a lot after that. I hadn't done anything dumb or made any huge mistakes, and the match was going well. It could always be better, of course, but I was calm and generally happy with how things were going. When we had two stages left, one of my friends told me where I stood in the results with almost certainty.

It was actually within my grasp to accomplish my goal for the match. I purposefully hadn't been paying attention to the scores, but now I knew, and there was no way I could go back to not knowing. My heart rate spiked. I logically thought about my performance up until that point, and I hadn't done anything "special" or "tried extra hard," and I was still winning. Wait, I was just shooting the targets the way I had trained myself to, and I was winning?

I truly believed in my heart that just shooting the targets and doing my best would give me the best score. I had tested it all summer in practice, and I knew it was true. That process that I believed in was now paying off in a match. I knew I would be happy with myself regardless of what the other competitors did if I could continue to perform in that way the rest of the match. All I had to do was continue to shoot the targets at my own pace and not push.

The last two stages were outstanding, or more precisely, they were exactly at my skill level. No more, no less. I accomplished my goal, and I felt like I found a big piece of the puzzle that I was missing. All I had to do was be myself at matches.

# CHAPTER 8
# INDOCTRINATING YOURSELF

A potent tool—maybe the most powerful tool—when it comes to combating pressure, is indoctrination. That is a powerful word that probably conjures up being in a cult for many of the readers, and that's exactly how I mean it. You can indoctrinate yourself with productive ideas until you believe them down to your core. It will make you a much stronger competitor, mentally.

You can spend your time in training believing you are fast enough to win, or believing that so long as you see your sight lift off the target you will be accurate enough. The possibilities are pretty much endless as far as what you can train yourself to believe. You need to train yourself to behave in a certain way in matches and to feel in your bones that if you behave the way you are supposed to, then you will get a good result in a match.

Most top shooters believe that they are good enough, that they can win, even that they SHOULD win. That level of confidence comes from training themselves (knowingly or unknowingly) that they are champions at heart and deserving of the win. This is the ultimate level of confidence.

The way to indoctrinate yourself in this manner is to pick out the thing you think you need to do in order to achieve some goal. What you need to do will vary depending on you and your goals, but try to think of some "big picture" sort of thing. Shooting in control, seeing your sights lift, training every day or whatever else you think you need to do would each make a good basis for your belief. A good example is "if I call every single shot in the match, then I will beat Dave." In this case, let's say that a shooter is always battling with some rival named Dave. Sometimes our hypothetical shooter rushes a little bit and then makes a mistake that swings the match in Dave's favor. Our shooter knows if he just doesn't do that one thing, he will beat his rival. He just needs to find a way to believe it and use that belief to drive the action he needs to take.

Once you have picked out the one thing you believe you need to do, you can confirm it for yourself. This could come from looking at match results, consulting with other shooters, or looking through training material. The idea is you need to believe with every part of yourself that if you do this one thing, then you are going to accomplish that goal. The process of convincing yourself never really stops; you keep seeking out more information and pushing yourself to believe this one idea.

Back to our hypothetical shooter, once he believes completely that he will beat Dave if he just makes sure to call every shot in the match, he's in a great place to actually pull it off. If any shadow of a doubt creeps in that something else is more important at some point during the match, then he didn't really believe it fully at the level necessary to ensure success.

From Joel:

I never thought I was fast enough. Even though people commented on how fast I was, I always thought I needed to be faster. I had a real eye-opener while I trained with Ben and shot drills next to him. I didn't beat him, but I learned that I'm not as slow as I thought I was. After several training experiences like that and comparing times, I got to the point that I actually believed in my heart that I was fast enough. Others could look at me like "duh, I already told you that months ago," but it was more meaningful that I believed it myself.

I attended a bowling pin match that I really wanted to win. The goal is to shoot your bowling pins off a table faster than the other person, and you are literally racing the person next to you. I had to shoot against some very fast shooters, and a lot of my peers were there. One person, in particular, was extremely fast. His best runs were near perfect, and in my mind, I thought I'd be happy with just matching him. I got more nervous the longer I watched him shoot. My friends are telling me how fast he is, and that I'll need to really be "on it" to beat him. Will he even have makeup shots when he's shooting against me? What will I do if he goes one for one on every pin?

Regardless of what I saw, I knew in my heart that I was fast enough. I do not need anyone else to confirm what I feel, and I don't even need to share my feelings. I believe it to be a fact. The other shooter is very fast, but so am I. When I shoot against him, I know in my heart I will win if I just use fundamentals and shoot the targets. I was not sharing any of my thoughts with others, it didn't matter what anyone else thought. Whether it's right or wrong, all that mattered is what I thought and believed.

There were twentyish people in a double elimination, best two out of three, match. I never lost a single round against some very talented shooters. No matter what I saw peripherally, or how fast I could hear the other person shooting, all I did was worry about what I was doing. I had to know, and believe, I was good enough to win. No one else could do it for me.

# PART 3
# VISUALIZATION

# CHAPTER 9

# WHAT IS VISUALIZATION?

Many people develop excellent shooting and movement skills throughout their training. They get a fast draw, explosive position changes, and rock-solid marksmanship fundamentals. However, there is a big difference between having amazing capabilities and actually utilizing those capabilities under pressure in a match.

The bridge between your skills and your performance is visualization. This section of the book will discuss in detail how this bridge functions and how to make it work for you, and we'll revisit visualization again a little later from a different perspective as well.

The most important thing that anyone can understand about this "bridge" between your skills and your match performance is that you can have all the skills in the world, but if you don't visualize properly executing the skills you have, you are going nowhere. The "bridge" could be described as the transmission in your car or the modem that connects your PC to the internet. It is absolutely critical to leveraging the skills you already have.

Visualization means creating images in your mind or recalling feelings. That's it. However, the images you create should be meaningful to you and allow you to recall them when it matters. During a stage walk through you memorize target placements and visual markers, so you know exactly how you are going to run the stage. It needs to be pointed out here that the exact picture in your mind and the exact elements you focus on will be a bit different for everyone. Maybe you like to think about specific spots in the center of each target, or perhaps you prefer to think in terms of shooting positions. It doesn't really matter how you do it, what matters is that you have a system that you can replicate at a match.

Visualizations are an extremely powerful tool. Consider the idea that it is impossible to excel in practical shooting without excellent visualization skills. These skills enable you to memorize and then execute a stage plan. It isn't enough to walk through the stage a couple of times to get a general idea of how it's laid out. You will not have precisely memorized target positions or shooting locations at this point, and you're going to be "flying blind' in the middle of the stage. You absolutely need to master visualization skills in order to develop solid stage plans. We'll cover detailed stage plan development a little later in more detail as well.

Let's take a step back from how visualization is used in matches and instead talk about how it gets developed during training and then applied in a match.

## Visualization in Practice

During your training, you are likely spending the majority of your time working on small and specific drills, simple drills where you are drawing, and shooting a bunch of rounds in just a few seconds. During your training, you develop skills like gripping your gun properly and firing quickly without pushing it around. During this process, you are going to learn about where you need to put your focus to get the result you desire.

As an example, let's say you are working on the classic Bill Drill. This is six shots at seven yards in under two seconds (hopefully). During your training, let's say you are a little bit slow on the draw, and maybe your firing hand is tensing up a lot and causing you to get trigger freeze. You probably know that feeling when your hand is so bound up and tense that your trigger finger doesn't release the trigger far enough to reset between shots, and you are unable to fire the gun quickly. Your Bill Drill might sound like Bop-Bop- . . . Bop-Bop-Bop-Bop. What happened on the third shot? We all know what happened: you got trigger freeze and were pulling a dead trigger that wasn't reset, then you had to hurry up and reset it to keep firing.

During your training, you focus on being more relaxed, and you get things dialed into where you can hit your goal Bill Drill time of two seconds with regularity. You might learn that if you exhale before the start signal, your body relaxes. You learn that if you stare a hole in the center of the "A Zone," then your gun will go precisely to that spot where you are looking on the draw. These things are what we would refer to as mental "cues." We'll be covering the use of mental and physical cues in your shooting and how they are used to form visualizations throughout this book, and this is a very important concept to internalize as you absorb all of this.

If you are shooting the Bill Drill and want that result, just call on the appropriate "cue" that helps drive the result. Looking at the spot you want to hit, getting your hand pressures correct, bringing your gun up on the way into a target, and so on are all potential cues. As you can probably see at this point, paying attention to cues and then using the right one at the right time can be quite helpful.

You will probably find that your brain is reliably able to do things for you without you consciously having to worry about the details. Once you have trained yourself to do any specific action, you simply call on the appropriate cue that drives it and then sit back and watch it happen. It is essential that you just let your body do what it has been trained to do and not try to interfere consciously. If you try to interfere with your training consciously, you end up trying to make something happen and that generally leads to mistakes.

# CHAPTER 10
# STAGE MEMORIZATION

One of the most obvious uses of your visualization skills is memorizing your plans for a stage. Let's say you have a stage that has you shooting from five different positions at nine targets and seven pieces of steel. You need to memorize a detailed plan of exactly where you are going, what the target engagement order is, and where the reload points are. Each detail of the stage needs to be committed to memory in order for the execution to be on point.

To remember your stage plan, you should memorize a picture of each task you need to complete, in the order you need to complete them. A mental image of each target/array, each shooting position, each reload, and any "waypoint" markers are all things you will need to memorize.

Good shooters will be able to close their eyes and see a movie of themselves working through the stage. They see a picture of each target and then see their sights come onto the target. They confirm the sight picture in a way that is appropriate for the difficulty of that particular target and then move on to the next thing. If you don't have a first-person movie (or slideshow) of you shooting the stage in your head, then you are not ready to shoot the stage. It is that simple (figure 4).

Something many shooters do to help with that process is to walk the stage and then close their eyes and see if they can do it all again by memory. After that test, they walk the stage again to see if they have any uncertainty about a target or position. After that, they visualize it again. The process repeats as many times as it takes until they know exactly where each target is, and they can execute the plan without any hesitation.

The idea that you are going to memorize the stage in detail so you can then execute the stage with zero hesitation is an alien concept to some people. If you want to be successful, your stage runs can't be performed flying by the seat of your pants, as you improvise a stage plan while keeping track of the number of rounds remaining in your magazine. What you want to do is methodically work through a predetermined stage plan. You shouldn't need to make decisions during a stage run any more complicated than "should I fire an extra shot on that target or not."

We've all seen someone get to the middle of a stage looking like they've completely forgotten what to do next. They might be looking around for targets, or maybe they had something happen they didn't expect, and it shakes them enough that they panic. Another common thing you might see is someone shoot an activator sequence exactly how they planned and then stand there admiring their work. It could not have gone more perfect in their eyes, and you see them stand there in amazement and happiness before their brain kicks in and they remember they still have the rest of the stage to shoot. Their whole focus was on not messing up the activation sequence they planned, and the rest of the stage was just an afterthought. Any scenario like this is just an indication that the stage plan had not been fully visualized.

1)

2)

3)

4)

5)

6)

7)

*Figure 4: Although a simple stage, you should be able to visualize all parts of the stage before you run it. 1) Draw to partial on right. 2) Engage partial on right. 3) Transition to partial on left. 4) Reload, while moving. 5) Engage open target right. 6) Poppers right to left. 7) Open target left to finish.*

## Cueing Your Stage Run

Cueing can be described as the physical part of stage memorization. As mentioned earlier, cues are specific to you, and they give you points to focus on that will help you achieve the result you want. You should plan the physical part of shooting during your walkthrough and use cues to remember it. You need to think about a position that you are going to drop step out of and think about how carefully pressing the trigger straight back feels for a tight partial or difficult shot. Focus on those specific types of items as you tell your body exactly how things should feel as you do your stage walk through.

Be sure to include mental notes in your visualization of anything you perceive as being particularly important for you. It could be making sure you are extra careful with the sights on a tight shot, remembering to run really hard to a specific position, not forgetting to reload in a particular spot, or keeping the gun up and snapping it from target to target as you move through an array. By knowing your own shooting, you'll know which things you could be prone to having issues with, and you can plan to shift your conscious attention around to those things at the right time on the stage.

1)

2)

*Figure 5: An example of cueing from the stage example above could be "Quick" for the reload and movement in 1). Then, "Gun up" prior to getting to 2) in order to get the gun up and on the open target. This will ensure you are ready to shoot as soon as you are coming into position and your sights clear the wall.*

## Running the Program

When you are within the next two to three shooters in the order, you should start visualizing the stage again. It's time to stop talking to your friends and get ready to perform. Apply a grip enhancer if you need it and make sure you have all your magazines on you and loaded. You should start walking the stage again when the shooter before finishes their run, and you are the "on deck" shooter. Make sure you are confident that you know where all the targets are, and you are ready to execute your plan without hesitation.

Your final walkthrough of the stage should really be just a formality to confirm what you already know. You should know the stage by heart and be very sure of what you are going to do. Pay attention to anything that strikes you as uncertain in your plan. It's not ideal to make any adjustments to your plan at this point, but if anything appears that it might be a problem you need to pay attention to that and do your best to account for it. For sure if you find this happens to you often, you need to refocus yourself on your walkthroughs to do a better job of making sure you have a solid plan.

## Reshooting a Stage

Sometimes you will need to "reshoot" a stage you previously had an attempt at. Reshoots are common enough that almost everyone who competes regularly has had to do it at some point. Ironically, even though you might assume that getting a second crack at a stage would likely produce an even better performance, the reality is often the opposite. Quite often, people curse the "reshoot gods" for poor performance on a reshoot. There is undoubtedly some mental management aspect to reshoots which warrants specific discussion.

The most important thing to remember about a reshoot is you need to treat it like a stage you've never shot before. Human nature might cause you to assume that since you just visualized and shot the stage a short time ago it should still be fresh in your mind and you don't need to repeat the whole process. But how many times have you heard jokes about reshoots not going well, or never going as well as the first run? Those issues are caused by not correctly visualizing and preparing for the second run on the stage. Simply having shot the stage once doesn't prepare you to do it again.

Your entire visualization process should start over if you have to reshoot a stage. Ask to be moved to the bottom of the shooting order so you have time to prepare. Start visualizing the stage again as if you've never shot it, several shooters before it's your turn. Think about where you want to move and where the targets will be, and be ready to execute without hesitation. Walk through the stage while the stage is being reset and you are the next shooter. You should not assume it will go well because you've shot it before.

You might be tempted to run a different plan than the first attempt, but in truth there are very few valid reasons you should consider making a change to your stage plan before a reshoot. The most common reason for a change is if your plan was significantly slower than the plan you observe other people executing. If there is a serious time advantage to changing plans, it may be worth switching. The other change you should consider making would be if you had a problem with an activator sequence. Maybe a popper falling was the activator for a swinger, and it fell really slow, so you decide to shoot it twice to make it fall faster. Maybe you felt really rushed on the timing for a sequence, and you choose to change your order to a less aggressive one. For the majority of reshoots however, if your original plan went reasonably well, you should not make any changes.

Especially, do not try to push harder than you did the first time, or treat it like the first attempt was a "warm-up" run. This is a very common error that comes naturally to many people, assuming that you can always do "better" the second time around. If you had a 5.8 hit factor the first time around, and your main rival who shot after you got a 6.2, you either consciously or unconsciously try to hit 6.3 on your reshoot. Reality will often smack you in the face in that case with a 5.2 after an unforced error delta or mike caused by you rushing parts of the stage. You should shoot it to your ability with the same level of focus as you did the first time you shot it. Give it the same respect you would give to a stage you've never shot before.

# CHAPTER 11
# VISUALIZATION EXERCISES

This section contains a series of specific training and match visualization exercises that should help you take your shooting to the next level. These exercises and concepts are things that I work with regularly.

## Training Cues

The most important tool in technical skill development is managing training cues properly. You might be wondering, what is a training cue, and how do you use it? We discussed training cues a little bit earlier, but this concept is critical to understand so we'll dive into more detail on it.

Let's take it from the top. People are terrible multi-taskers on a conscious level. You can subconsciously have your heart pump, breathe, digest food, and so forth. All of those bodily functions are generally handled without any conscious intervention or even awareness on your part. However, you can occasionally shift your attention (your conscious attention) to one aspect of your body's activity and exert some control over it. You can think about your breathing, for example, and then consciously control exactly when and how deeply you breathe. But you can't consciously control all of your bodily functions at the same time, the mind can really only focus on one thing at a time.

When you are executing your shooting ability on a stage or in training, you generally are not going to consciously control any piece of that. Of course, when first learning something new you need to control EVERY piece consciously. But once you train to the point of subconscious competence, then there isn't any reason to "think your way through" things any longer.

Let's look at a brief example to explain this a little bit more fully. If you are at the range working on the classic Bill Drill, and you have never fired a gun previously, you are going to be consciously thinking through every piece of that exercise. (If you aren't aware, a Bill Drill is shooting six shots into the A zone of a target 7 yards away as quickly as you can. The details of that aren't crucial for the purposes of this example, just know that it is one of the simplest drills that anyone can dream up.)

On your first day shooting a gun, you are going to need to think about each piece in detail. Imagine you got a safety briefing from a competent instructor, and some technical training as well . . . but that's it. You have never actually shot before. And here you are, now you are shooting a Bill Drill. When you go to draw your pistol at the start of the drill you probably will need to think about where your holster is and find the correct hand position on the gun. You need to consciously clear your holster while keeping your finger off the trigger, disengage your gun's safety (if it has one), and double check your hand position on the gun so you don't lose control of it. After that's done you line up the sights on the target with equal height and equal light, just like you were instructed. You haven't even fired a shot yet and you are working through all of these details, step by step. Without having any subconscious training experience to draw upon, you have no choice but to think through every step and direct it consciously.

After you train for a while, you will get to the point of unconscious competence with certain tasks. Think about the way you drive your car around town. You can probably carry on a conversation with a passenger as you smoothly negotiate corners, change lanes, and so on. You don't need to think about any of those specific tasks. You aren't thinking about the turn indicator . . . you just put on your signal before you take a corner.

Shooting works the same way as driving or anything else. Eventually, you get to that point of subconscious competence. In terms of shooting training, I would say that after some amount of training you become a machine that shoots. That isn't a good or a bad thing; everyone trains habits, and to some extent just do the things they do after a while. Practice makes things permanent. At this point in your training when you are executing most things subconsciously, you are ready to benefit from training cues.

If you continue to look at your shooting as a machine (for better or worse), then think of the training cue as you intervening in the machine and trying to change the way the machine operates. Maybe you have decided that you have insufficient grip pressure with your support hand. A training cue you might use is "crush" when you draw the gun and put your support hand on it. You are consciously forcing that hand to add more pressure.

Over time, if you consistently apply a training cue you can expect your subconscious technique to begin to change. It takes a lot of time and repetition, but eventually you will be able to change your shooting. Just think how you've managed to internalize and subconsciously do things like drawing a gun efficiently and consistently compared to when you first started.

The main thing to understand here is that you can only have conscious intervention in one thing at a time. It is difficult to have more than one training cue effectively utilized in the same exercise. Maybe if it is a complicated exercise, you can do a couple different cues if they are separate activities with a time gap between them. Maybe one cue for the reload and another cue when you shoot while you are moving on the same drill or something like that would work . . . but generally, it is just one cue at a time.

There is another interesting bit about training cues to understand, and that is the individuality aspect. What a particular cue means to one shooter will mean something else entirely to another shooter. "Relax" is a pretty good example of one of those cues. Depending on the person and the context it could mean a lot of different things. "Relax" to one guy means slumping his shoulders a little bit. To another guy, it means stop "death gripping" the gun with the firing hand and inducing trigger freeze. It really depends on the person. Keep this in mind when someone offers you advice.

The important thing for an individual to figure out is what cue (input) produces what action (output). Once you start to learn yourself, you can start applying the right cue at the right time in your training, and you can really build yourself into a better machine.

### Training Visualization

Probably the most critical visualizations you are going to do are "pre-stage" visualizations. These are the visualizations that are essentially programming yourself to run the stage. Understand that this is a process that is not normally present during training specifically, meaning you don't typically visualize a drill before shooting it. However, the manner in which you train yourself to visualize during training will directly affect your ability to use the skill when visualizing a stage. And there are certainly some shooters who DO visualize some training drills before shooting them. If you find this is helpful for you, by all means use that as a tool.

During your training, you build technical shooting skills. You hold the gun like this, pull the trigger like that, and move this way. The list of skills you can build up in your training is long. However, each skill is best trained as a small piece of a larger puzzle. When you work on reloading, you don't need to do it in the context of shooting a training stage. You can just break that skill out into its own little drill.

Training is typically going to be done without having much of an element of memorization or punishment. Let me explain what that means a little bit.

Most people train on drills or simple exercises. You tend to have a small number of targets that you shoot in one order or another. You do lots of repetition of shooting to build up your core skills. There isn't a need to memorize a 32-round long course where you have more than a dozen targets, in addition to multiple shooting positions. People just don't train that way. To be honest, they shouldn't train that way even if they could, because it is inefficient to train that way if you are trying to address relatively simple shooting issues. All of the setup and reset time required for this destroys training efficiency.

Training also happens without you being "punished" as much as you are in a match. I don't mean physical punishment, but rather social and emotional types of consequences are more powerful in matches than in practice. In practice, you can make mistakes without any real consequences. This is the way training has to be, otherwise it is going to be challenging to try out new things and really improve your shooting. Once you get to a match, things are much different.

## Match Visualization

At a match, there is a memorization and planning element not usually present in practice, and the results of your shooting really start to matter. Your first "on demand" run on a stage is the one that gets recorded for a score. Whatever you think you can do based on your training, or however good you think you are, doesn't really matter. You don't get scored that way, you get scored based upon what you actually do.

What proper pre-stage visualizations do is take care of the memorization element of the stage and prepare you mentally to shoot "for real."

Imagine going through a stage "blind," a stage for which you have never seen the layout. When you get the start beep, a blindfold is taken off your head, and you need to GO. You start figuring out what targets you need to shoot and where you need to go. You would probably do this as you are drawing your gun and bringing it up. There would be lots of little moments of indecision. Can you see these targets from over here or over there? Did you already shoot that target? Is there anything to shoot through this window? Moving through a stage "blind" involves a lot of quick decision making.

Obviously, shooting a stage blind is going to take more time because all of the decisions you need to make take lots of time to sort out in your head. Even if you are a "blind stage master" and train yourself to shoot blind stages all the time, you are still going to be quite a bit faster if you get to look at the stage ahead of time.

Earlier we referred to visualization as the bridge between your skills and your performance. On a "blind" stage you don't get to visualize any of it ahead of time, so you get no benefit of having burned some elements of the stage into memory so you can execute them subconsciously. When you get to walk through the stage before shooting, instead of making decisions on the fly you can visualize the way you want to shoot the stage and program that in ahead of time. You cut out conscious decision making entirely from the process because everything is decided beforehand. You can even work some "cues" into your plan for the parts of the stage you consider to be tricky. "Feel the trigger reset" if that suits you on the "hard" shots on a stage. If you have trouble forcing yourself to run at truly top speed, and you have a 15-yard movement element on a stage, maybe you cue yourself to "run your lungs out." In any event, you program your stage run in, using cues when they are helpful.

When you visualize a stage, there are a few rules to follow:

1. Be specific
2. Be detailed
3. Call on your training
4. Know when you are ready

1. You should understand that when you visualize a stage run, you are calling on the training you have already done. You are calling on the skills you already have. You can even think of specific performance on a particular day and think about recreating exactly what you did on another occasion. Maybe you have one shooting position on a stage 10 yards away from the next position. You can visualize a drill you were running a few weeks prior during your training that looks similar. The approach you had at that time, and the training cue you used, will get you the same result on match day if you think back and recall those things specifically.

2. You need to be detail-oriented when it comes to visualization, and it is vital to be as specific as possible about what you want. Your brain is a powerful tool, but you need to visualize exactly what you want to do and not leave anything out so your brain can do its job to recall those details. Your brain CAN provide the right outputs if you provide the right inputs to it. If you're going to come into a position gun up and ready to go, and then stop with your feet spread apart wide as you engage the partial target behind the wall, then you need to specifically program each and every step of that process during your stage

visualization. If you just think "go over there and shoot that thing" then you will get exactly that. Maybe you won't like how your feet set up when you stop in position, or perhaps you will be late to get the gun up and ready to go. Anything can happen because you didn't program the specific details into your brain.

3. During your stage visualizations, you call on technical skills you've developed during your training. If you are not well trained in doing something, meaning that you are not subconsciously competent at doing a specific task, then I would consider that thing off the table for a match. Don't try to do it. For example, if you need to consciously manage to put down a foot and then fire a shot as you shoot on the move, then I wouldn't really recommend trying to put that into action in a match.

4. One of the more common failings that people have during the stage visualization process is not knowing when they are done. The rule is simple: When you can see the whole stage from start to finish in your mind without hesitation, then you are ready. Any little mental hiccup or moment where you need to think about what you are doing is potentially going to be a problem for you when you are running the stage live. Be sure that you have this process down and you can see the stage completely before you consider the visualization complete.

# CHAPTER 12
# MANAGING STRESS

Competitive shooting is a high-stress endeavor, much like any other competitive event. However, some stress is good for you. You want to be at a place of "optimal" readiness. A little bit of stress is going to help you do that. Think about it like this: On the spectrum of human stress level there is everything from groggy, to alert, to "keyed up," to panic. You want to be somewhere more toward the middle of that spectrum and not at either extreme.

## Stress Up

It is occasionally useful to increase the amount of stress you are under at a match in order to get yourself into the optimal zone. Think about an example five stages into your club match, shooting with all your buddies. It can turn into a pretty low-stress environment where you aren't terribly invested in the results, and not really doing your best.

To maximize your score, you probably need to increase the stress level in those situations so that your brain is fully engaged in your success. There are plenty of good ways to do that.

In low-stress matches, squadding with a rival shooter of similar ability can help keep you focused and motivated to do your best. Maybe neither of you have a real chance to win the match, but between you, the competition is generally excellent. That is absolutely a dynamic upon which you can capitalize to improve your performance, and really one of the key ways for most shooters to stay engaged in a match that they aren't going to win. If you are in C-Class, B-Class, etc. having the inter-class rivalries and competition going at your club match is a great way to ensure you stay fully invested in your match results.

You might also be able to increase the stress by watching a shooter who is actually below your skill level, especially if they are shooting well. You can watch someone shoot a stage with quite an excellent run but understand at the same time that you should be able to do even better. This can definitely help increase the stress level for most people.

Setting small goals for yourself at a match is also an excellent way to put some pressure on. Maybe setting the goal of zero miss/no-shoot penalties for your club match helps apply some pressure on you to pay attention to details during your walkthrough, and make sure you aren't slacking off on the preparation. Verbalizing this goal to other people can help hold you accountable for it. It is an excellent tool to get invested in the match and stay invested.

## Stress Down

Most of the time, when people want to manipulate their stress level, they are interested in reducing the amount of stress that they are under. I have seen more times than I can count someone exhibiting the signs of too much stress and then immediately having a bad performance. Shaky hands, trouble making decisions, trembling, hypervigilance, and so on are the signs of too much stress. This stuff is typical before the first stage of a big match, or a stage that a shooter finds particularly challenging.

If you recognize the signs of too much stress building up, or you are coming up to a stage that you know will stress you, you should begin taking specific steps to reduce your stress level.

Controlling your breathing is a valuable tool for lowering stress and is actually one of the easiest techniques to use. You don't want to be all keyed up standing there hyperventilating while you wait to shoot. People tend to take lots of rapid shallow breaths when they are freaking out. You want to do the opposite by following these instructions:

1. Inhale slowly and deeply through your nose. Keep your shoulders relaxed. Your abdomen should expand, and your chest should rise very little.
2. Exhale slowly through your mouth. As you blow air out, purse your lips slightly, but keep your jaw relaxed. You may hear a soft "whooshing" sound as you exhale.
3. Repeat this breathing exercise for several minutes.

There are other ways you can reduce stress as well. One method that works really well is to take a look around and notice signs of stress in other people. You might see people being indecisive about stage plans (when they usually are not) or making comments about the stage being challenging. You might see people with the shakes a little bit.

In any event, recognizing the signs that other people are stressed typically helps mitigate the stress you feel. Other people are having a tough time too, and seeing that can be very helpful.

Another good way to deal with early match stress is to develop stage plans that you consider very simple or easy. You don't want to make a tough situation even tougher for yourself by running complicated or risky stage plans. After you knock out a couple of decent stages and your stress level dissipates, then you should be fine.

A helpful tool to use during training for many people is to recall a moment of particular match stress. You can think about your first stage at your first Nationals or even your first stage ever. One of those examples usually does the trick. Everyone has moments in their shooting career that tested them, so just imagine one of yours. The feelings you felt during that time can be called back to the front of your mind, and you can experience those same feelings again. This is very helpful because it gives you a chance to run visualizations of some shooting tasks while you are experiencing past match stress.

Remembering stressful match situations is a great tool to use in your training. Say you set up an exercise, and before you shoot it for the first time you recall some moment of match pressure and bring that feeling to the forefront of your mind and body. Your heart rate should elevate a bit, and you are right back into whatever situation you are thinking of. Then run visualizations of the drill and shoot the drill. That first "cold" run is an excellent simulation of match pressure.

### Recall Good Performance (Confidence Builder)

If you are struggling during your training, it may help to recall a past successful stage or training session. Remember the calm you likely felt before you shot some stage, and then the way you tracked your sights perfectly and shot the stage of your life. Remember the happiness you felt afterward.

Again, taking thirty seconds or a minute and doing proper visualization of a past "good" performance can help you perform better in the moment. This is especially useful during times of challenging training or when you are having some other sort of problem. Thinking of times you had struggles and then overcame them can return you to that state of mind.

### Calm Problem Solving

The ideal mindset to have as a shooter is one of calm and professional problem-solving. The mark of an excellent shooter is when they are not doing very well on a stage, you really wouldn't know it from watching their body language. Maybe they have an extra shot over here, and a gun malfunction over there, but as you watch the shooter on the stage they don't act like anything bad is going on. They just move from one thing to the next.

When you see a shooter who isn't as good start having issues on a stage, the panic is often visible in everything they do. They start rushing from one task to the next and back again, because usually they need to fix some other mistake they made. You see their eyes move around frantically, because they start getting ahead of themselves and aren't sure where they are in the stage and what they are actually doing. In this case, the anxiety is clearly visible.

During your training and matches, you should strive to have a mindset of calm problem-solving. One thing at a time. Step by step. You are paying attention, but not panicking. You are pushing hard, but not rushing. You are fast, but not rushed. It is something that takes quite a lot of time and experience to master.

# PART 4
# BUILDING YOUR MATCH MINDSET

# CHAPTER 13
# BRING YOUR MATCH ATTITUDE

The attitude you bring to a match is important. The way you show up (mentally) to the match will determine if you shoot a score in the match that you are happy with, or not. You can show up having done the preparation necessary to be in a good head space and shoot to your best ability . . . or not. That is entirely up to you.

Ben's First National Title:

Winning my first national title in USPSA was essentially the result of indoctrinating myself to execute my shooting strategy while ignoring what everyone else was doing.

After a few years on the super squad, it became apparent to me that "racing" with the other shooters on the squad was not something productive for me to do, especially at that time in my career. In a high-pressure situation like shooting Nationals, all the top contenders are always in a battle to be in the lead. This battle lasts for days on end and is very taxing for everyone.

I knew that I wasn't as fast as the other guys, and my only chance to win would be to avoid mistakes and avoid racing. I trained myself for months to ignore everyone else's time and points as they shot stages. I wouldn't even watch the top guys shoot. I looked at the ground. My theory at that time was that if the other guys shot a perfect match, there was zero chance of me winning. I accepted that. I also recognized that if other people made mistakes, my best hope of winning was to shoot my own match.

On the morning of the third day, after some mistakes from other people, I found myself in the lead of the match. This was after two days of completely ignoring what everyone else was doing and focusing on my own shooting. This put me in a position that I had not adequately prepared myself for mentally. That situation was being in the lead at Nationals. It might sound strange to some, but it can cause crushing amounts of pressure to be in the lead. Stage after stage goes by, and the match winds down. If you are in the lead going into the last stage, you may be thinking, "Shoot this stage without screwing up, and you win." The pressure for me was incredible. I think it took five years off my life.

## Understand the Test

To get your head right for a match, you absolutely need to understand the test that you will be subjected to. Maybe "understand" isn't even the right word. An intellectual understanding of the test is easy. Really having experienced the test, and having self-awareness during the test so you can do better the next time, is the type of understanding I am referring to. You need to feel the crushing pressure of your desire to do well coming into contact with the moment you need to make it happen. Once you know what I am talking about, then you understand the test the way you need to understand it. That might come across as heavy, but it is absolutely accurate. This is a concept that the more advanced level shooters will likely have felt at some point or will feel. If you are a new shooter in D-Class, this is a bit over your head at this point.

When you go to a match, you are going to be tested on your ability to shoot fast and accurately, while under pressure. The more you care, the more pressure there is. The more you train, the more pressure you bring with you. The more you win, the more you are expected to win. The list goes on forever, but the "fast and accurate shooting" is only the beginning of the way you are going to be tested. There is a big difference between laying down a fast drill run for Instagram with unlimited attempts, and shooting "for real" for the title. Don't get these two situations confused.

# CHAPTER 14

# HIGH PRESSURE ENVIRONMENT?

If you have been to USPSA Nationals, then you likely have some understanding of a high-pressure environment. Even if you are shooting in a group where nobody in the squad has a realistic chance of winning anything, you will notice that everyone takes the match more seriously than other matches. There is nothing structurally different about Nationals, it is just stages set up in various bays, and you rotate around and shoot them in turn. The stages are generally unremarkable as USPSA stages go. There might be a couple that are super hard or interesting, but most of the stages are just . . . stages.

The reason that people take the match more seriously is that this is the one match that matters the most to USPSA shooters for the entire season. Each division will have a National Champion. I can confirm to you that being USPSA National Champion doesn't really do a whole lot for your life. You don't get a big check, and you certainly aren't going to impress members of the opposite sex. Nobody outside of USPSA cares all that much. But internally . . . it is a big deal. I didn't sleep for forty-eight hours after winning my first title because I just didn't even know what to do with my life anymore. With something like that on the line, everyone takes things seriously.

The bigger the match, the more the pressure. The more the pressure builds, the more people tend to crack under it and make mistakes. It is that simple.

## Control What You Can Control

A huge part of successful practical shooting competition is understanding what is within your control, what isn't, and acting accordingly. I don't think most people have a tough time understanding these things; it is not hard to figure that stuff out. Here's a simple a list of control items that I prepared:

Things you cannot control:

- Other competitors' shooting ability
- Range officers on a stage
- The way the stages are built
- The weather
- Whatever is going on in your personal life at that moment

Things you can control:

- You

Ok, so this is kind of a cheeky way to make a point that most people should understand already. You only control you. Your actions are going to determine your score. If something someone else does changes your score, then you can't really control that anyway.

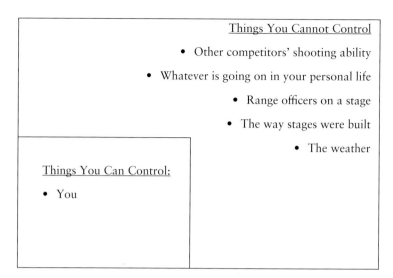

Figure 6: There will be many things happening at a match; however, there is only one thing that you can control.

With the obvious stuff out of the way, we can move on to the not obvious stuff. The hard part about "understanding what is within your control, what isn't, and acting accordingly" is the last part. Controlling your behavior so you are focused on what you are doing is very challenging at a big match. There are so many moving pieces and so many things happening all at once that it is tough not to focus on things (such as other peoples' shooting) that absolutely are not going to help you.

Essentially, in your battle to devote your mental energy to productive things like stage visualization and gear checking or anything that is going to help you, it is almost impossible not to get caught up in unproductive stuff that wastes your energy. The main idea here is to minimize those distractions and keep your eye on the ball.

There will be lots more on this in the "squadding" section.

# CHAPTER 15

# KNOW YOURSELF

The key to managing yourself is knowing yourself. You need to understand your own tendencies and work with that information to set yourself up for the best possible result. If I walk into a room with donuts on a table, it is highly likely that I am going to eat one . . . or two . . . or more. I know that about myself. So, if I need to be cutting weight, I just try not to be put into a situation where there are donuts on the table.

In matches, the opportunities to trip yourself up are almost endless. You can get sucked into paying attention to a plethora of problems that other people are having. You can get involved in conversations that are interesting but don't really have anything to do with the match. If you are reading this book, you are probably more serious about your shooting than most people at a club level event. Just in the interest of camaraderie and friendship, most people are happy to chat you up, and many of them won't care about their match performance as much as you do. This is fine to some degree, but bear in mind it is up to you to manage those interactions and assert yourself when it is time to direct your attention elsewhere.

You should know if you benefit from watching your direct competitors shoot or not, and act accordingly. If, for example, you get intimidated or nervous when watching your biggest rival shoot, then you might be best off squadding apart or just not paying attention when that person shoots. If you are motivated and energized by watching your rival shoot, then act accordingly. As you compete more and more, pay attention to the feelings and thoughts that you have when you are at matches. Those inner thoughts and feelings are speaking to you, and you should definitely listen.

## Have a Routine

You would be well served to develop a systematic routine for how you deal with matches. That process is vital to your long-term performance. The process from checking your equipment, to walking through stages, to visualization, to shooting a stage, all need to be systematic and trained into your approach. By consciously deciding how these actions are going to be done and training yourself accordingly, you are going to be positioned well to produce a consistent performance at your matches. You should be able to avoid significant logistical errors, like forgetting to fill magazines all the way, or forgetting about a target on a stage, these things should virtually never happen. Mistakes like this will happen on occasion for many of us . . . but it really should be a once a season or once every other season type of thing. If you are regularly having massive failures in your preparation, then that is a grave issue that you need to address promptly.

Most people have a habit or process for their "Make Ready." The main thing to accomplish is helping them relax and get comfortable while they perform their routine checklist. If you watch closely, you will notice some competitors always draw the gun and check their red dot brightness first thing, they seat the mag in the exact same way, they load the gun by pinching the forward cocking serrations between their thumb and index finger, they press check by moving their support hand under the dust cover and using the forward cocking serrations again, they apply the thumb safety/de-cock the gun and holster in roughly the same order and way. That person is checking everything as they calm down and get ready for the stage, and they are less likely to forget something like chambering the gun or turning on their red dot. You don't have to follow that exact routine as it is described, but it is helpful for you to have some sort of routine of your own.

Routine is something that you should be conscious of during your training and know that it can help you. This is where you practice and develop your standard mental processes. It is a natural thing that people change focal points and processes during training from one particular thing to another thing, as they train on different skills. It is important to be aware of what focal points and little mental checks work for you and work them into your routine.

From Ben:

The most important part of my "make ready" routine is the feel of my pistol in the holster. I like to have a firing grip on the gun as I re-holster the gun after loading it. I feel my thumb on top of my safety. I feel the meat of my hand up into the backstrap. The grip should feel perfect. I know that if I just recreate that feeling after the buzzer sounds, then I will build my grip correctly and be set up for a good stage. I can combine this feeling of a perfect grip with any last bit of visualization I might do.

# CHAPTER 16

# MATCH STRATEGY

The strategy you approach a match with is going to have a substantial effect on your outcome. Are you going to dominate the match, winning every stage? Are you going to leave people impressed with your speed? Are you going to cruise through the event dropping very few points? Are you going to squad with a rival and race with them on the stages?

For most people, the most effective way to get the best score is to essentially not be thinking about competing with the other shooters at the match. That might sound a bit silly, so it requires a bit of clarification. Nothing good happens for most people's performance when they pay attention to what other people are doing. This is true of almost any new or unskilled shooter. Racing with the pack tends to induce mistakes and frustration.

For more advanced shooters, there is going to be a little bit of the "race" element to their shooting. They often squad with rival shooters and go head-to-head from stage to stage. At most clubs, the top few guys have a healthy competition as they battle for setting high hit factors and fast stage times. This is good fun at club events. At larger matches, this same mentality, when put under major match stress, can lead to an implosion. Nothing good at all happens to these personalities when the major match pressure element gets added in.

Top tier super squad-level guys tend to be extremely competitive with one another but also have excellent self-awareness about the level of pressure they are likely to be feeling at different points in the match. They take it easy on stages when they are having pressure (such as the first stage of a championship). They push hard and try to dominate on stages that suit their skills, and the stages on which they feel confident.

It is important to pay attention to yourself as you start shooting matches. How do you feel? What is the pressure doing for you? When you "push" to set fast times, what is the outcome? Adopt the correct strategy for yourself, and don't let anyone influence you differently.

## Common Situations

Even the most well-prepared shooter is going to find themselves in challenging situations from time to time. What you consider challenging or what situations require special effort from you to keep under control is personality driven. As usual, self-awareness during competition is your ally. It will make you better over time. You don't want to be the guy who falls into the same behavioral patterns, time and time again, and never seems to learn lessons from past mistakes.

You will usually not be the fastest shooter in your squad. That isn't necessarily a bad thing. The winner of a match is the person who shoots the best. Speed is an essential component of that, but it doesn't determine everything. The challenge for many is watching someone shoot a stage a little bit faster than they can shoot it and then not doing anything about it. The temptation to push or race is genuine in high-pressure situations. It is generally counterproductive to try to push yourself past your known comfortable skill level. It can be helpful to develop a training partner who shoots faster than you or shoots a faster division than you. This can help you get used to accepting that you won't always be the fastest, but the best thing to do in the middle of actual competition is to shoot your own game and not someone else's.

Occasionally you will have a bad stage; everyone does from time to time. The degree of "bad" depends a bit on your level as a shooter. A top shooter taking a penalty on a stage is bad. A new shooter forgetting their stage plan entirely and backtracking to pick up targets they forgot is bad. These things happen. The strongest defense against these situations is proper preparation before the match even starts.

It helps to take a look at the match summary for top shooters at big matches like nationals. You will notice that even the very best have bad stages and still end up winning the match. You should mentally prepare yourself to shoot a good match. A good match sometimes includes terrible stages. That is the way it is. What you don't want to do is beat yourself up over a mistake or try to "catch up" to other people. Pushing to gain the ground you just lost due to a mistake usually compounds your problems.

Sometimes a couple bad stages turn into a bad match. Bad matches happen for everyone now and again. Everyone has days where they just aren't feeling it, nothing seems to go perfect, and the shooting is choppy. It absolutely happens to everyone. What you should do is try to take the match one stage at a time, do your best with what remains, and learn whatever lessons you can. You can't fix it in the moment. You will probably be mad. All of those feelings are normal. It is what you do afterward that is important. The best thing you can do is take your lessons on board and hit the training range with renewed vigor.

Major matches usually include a break for lunch that can sometimes trip people up. Lots of people mentally check out of the match and go eat a big meal. They come back sluggish and unfocused. You don't want that to be you! Obviously, some people don't have problems managing a lunch break, but many people do have those issues. There are some strategies that can help.

If the weather is ok, you might just want to stay out on the range where you have your next stage. Sit and chat with some buddies and snack a little bit. Take a close look at your next stage. Mentally keep yourself on the range and in the match, rather than treating it like a break from the match. This strategy is helpful for many.

You might find it helpful to walk to the upcoming stages and take a look at them. This can help you answer questions you may have about how to shoot them or give you other information about the stages you have coming up soon. You may want to check over your gear. Maybe you have a gun that needs its magazines cleaned frequently to be reliable, or something like that. Lunchtime is an excellent time to make everything perfect.

You may want to treat the stage after lunch as a "cold" stage. Pretend you weren't shooting all morning and take things a little bit easy. Confirm good sight pictures and shoot good point, basically treat it like a new day of shooting.

Maybe going to the safe area and doing a few dry draws and mag changes (with empty mags of course) helps get your mind and muscles back into the groove. Learn what you need to do to get back "in the zone" after a break and use smaller matches as a place to experiment so you know what works for you at major ones.

If you have a multi-day match, you should probably consider the upcoming days of competition at the end of a day. It is nice to take a walk through the stages you will shoot the next day and start mentally preparing yourself for what will be upcoming. You might also develop some questions to ask people who shot those stages already. Things like "what is the timing on that mover?" or "how were people running that stage?" are good things to find out if you can the day before.

# PART 5
# MATCH
# PREPARATION

# CHAPTER 17

# WHAT'S THE TEST?

Before you can prepare for a match, you need to understand what a match tests. That may seem obvious to you, but I can assure you most people don't have a complete understanding of what is being tested. As your experience and knowledge about practical shooting grows, this will become clear.

A match is a test of technical ability, equipment, and strategy under pressure. A lot of people are only really paying attention to the technical ability and equipment parts of the equation. They do not understand the strategy or the pressure element. This section will discuss each piece of this in detail. You, of course, can do very well at big matches without proper preparation. You can even win. You will not be able to win consistently unless you pay attention to each piece very carefully to build an effective process.

Obviously, the most significant component of performance in a shooting match is your technical shooting ability. Most of your score is going to hinge on this component. Your shooting ability is going to be developed through consistent and substantial practice. Of course, this is the one thing that isn't being discussed in this text. If you found your way to this book, inevitably you are aware of the amount of material available on both live and dry fire training to develop fast and consistent gun handling and effective shooting skills. You need to do that work over a long period of time in order to acquire the skills you are going to put to use on match day. Once you have acquired a certain level of technical ability, the mental game will become more and more important. At the top levels of the sport every competitor has solid technical skills, so the mental game largely determines who wins or loses.

### Using Cues

What you will need to pay careful attention to during your technical training are the cues that you are using to get the desired outcome. Those are the things that you will need to be visualizing when you are actually at a match shooting a stage. We introduced these types of training cues earlier in the training visualization section.

As an example, I find that if I feel my dominant hand thumb land on top of the safety of my gun while I am drawing the gun from the holster, I will have a correct grip as the gun comes up. Under match conditions (pressure), I call on that mental training cue to get the grip that I need on the gun in order to shoot effectively.

You should show up to a match with mental cues that you can call on during a stage walkthrough to get any necessary skill to manifest itself. It doesn't matter that much what the cues are, it just matters that you understand them, and you remember to put them into effect at the match.

Some examples of cues that I use are:

Look at the center of the steel target when you aim at it, do not look at the entire piece of steel as a target.

Look at the exact spot you want your foot to land until you are sure you have that spot nailed.

Stop your vision on the close target, so your gun doesn't keep moving through it.

It really doesn't matter what cue you use, but you need to use the correct cue to get the desired outcome. Many shooters build technical skills in practice and then never actually use them during a real match because they aren't doing detailed visualizations of their practice cues during an actual match.

If you don't fully understand everything related to this yet, go back and re-read the information presented about using cues in the "visualization" section. These cues are the key to tying together what you have built for skills during practice into your actual match performance.

## Equipment Preparation

Another piece of match preparation is making sure your equipment is ready to go. You should have a gun that you know is 100 percent reliable. You should have a backup gun that you are just as certain functions properly, but maybe you like it a bit less than the main gun. You should have ample ammunition similarly tested. You should have ancillary gear (belt, holster, etc.) that you are sure is in good working order. You should have any other bit of equipment that you might need. Everything from water to sunblock, to food. During match day, you should absolutely never want for anything. As the saying goes, better to have and not need than to need and not have. We will cover detailed information on each one of these points in the "Equipment" section.

### Understanding Match Strategy

A large part of how well you do in a match comes down to understanding and implementing proper match strategy for the given match. This means you need to understand scoring. You need to understand the complicated series of cause-and-effect relationships between how you choose to attack a shooting challenge (think of this as your input), and what kind of score that will generate (the output) over a series of attempts (average). Shooting is not as simple as "go do your best." You might be the fastest and best technical shooter around with the hottest Instagram practice videos, but if you aren't able to understand fundamental issues about how to approach shooting challenges, you will be at a disadvantage come match day.

Match strategy really just means you understand the test you are taking, and you optimize your inputs to give you the best average output. A little later in the "match strategy" section, we will cover these issues in detail.

The factor that gets the least discussion is typically that of pressure. In my opinion, the pressure element is significant enough that if it was removed from matches, we would have an entirely different set of people winning major matches regularly. The same group of guys would be on the super squads for their respective divisions, but different people would regularly be at the top. It is that important.

You aren't just being tested on your raw shooting ability, you need to manifest your ability under pressure on stages that you normally haven't seen or shot before. In order to win a big title, you need to maintain a high level of performance on stages like this over the course of multiple days. The better you do, the more the pressure builds. The more training you invest into the sport, the more the pressure builds.

I have seen seasoned professional shooters with their hands shaking before they start a stage. I have seen guys vomit in the bushes because the pressure makes them sick. Even pros lose IQ points like crazy when the pressure is on. Understanding match pressure will inform your training and strategy decisions and will help you optimize your outcome.

# CHAPTER 18
# PRE-MATCH RECON

Researching the match ahead of time is a smart way of preparing yourself. If the match is at the same location as the previous year, there's a pretty good chance it will have the same flavor. Watching YouTube videos from the previous matches should give you a pretty good idea of what to expect. Another option is talking to people who have shot that match previously. The match can change from year to year, but more than likely it will be similar if it's the same crew setting it up.

People get too caught up in studying the matchbook. The stages on the ground rarely look the same due to space or prop considerations. The people setting up the stage may have a different idea than the person who designed it. As such, it's a bad idea to start making stage plans off the diagrams. When you look at the matchbook, the main elements to pay attention to are things that appear out of the ordinary. Things like different starting positions, unloaded starts, single-hand shooting, swingers, etc. might be something you want to dedicate a little extra practice time to in the last few sessions before the match. Another good example would be looking at a matchbook and noticing there will be lots of partials with hardcover, or maybe there is a swinger on every stage, or there is a lot of weak hand shooting. It's good to identify anything you aren't comfortable with early so you can train on it before the match.

### Eating and Hydration

From Joel:

I am not a nutritionist, but here is a system that works for me.

During hot weather, I start hydrating the day before the match. If you start hydrating when you arrive at the match, you will just be battling to stay ahead of dehydration. A good rule of thumb is to drink at least one bottle of water per stage, some people may drink more. Even if you feel great or aren't thirsty, the key is to keep drinking. Once you start feeling not so great or get too hot, it will be a fight until the end of the day to get your body cooled back down and hydrated.

Drink your normal amount of caffeine. If you usually have a cup of coffee first thing in the morning, you should do the same thing on match day. Drink energy drinks or soda the same as you usually would. On that same note, do not decide match day is the day you want to try one of the energy drinks your friend has been telling you about.

I eat a regular dinner the night before the match, and I recommend sticking to your usual breakfast routine on match day. Once you get to the match, I recommend snacking throughout the day but never eating a large meal. You should never be hungry and never feel really full. I like to snack on things like jerky, almonds, mixed nuts, protein bars, and fruit. I rarely suggest eating the match lunch because it's usually very heavy food, and I do not want to feel so tired like I could take a nap afterward.

# CHAPTER 19

# EQUIPMENT

Practical shooting matches test the preparation of your equipment. In many instances, it is better to not think about it as testing to see who has the best gun, but rather think of a shooting match as testing to see if you prepared your equipment as a professional would. Your gun needs to run, consistently. It must 100 percent comply with the rules of your division, and it will likely be checked at larger matches. Your ammunition needs to be of the proper power factor and must hit consistently. You must have correct eyewear for the lighting conditions and so on. If you do not test your equipment, then you are leaving things to chance and eventually that is going to catch up with you. We all know more than one person with a gun that never runs. You don't want to be that person.

This section will explore the ins and outs of equipment preparation so you can give yourself the best possible chance of having properly functional gear. Note that it is phrased as "best chance" for a reason. Even if you are careful about checking your equipment and ensuring proper function and reliability, occasionally things are still going to go wrong. That is part of life and part of the game, but you want to keep that possibility to an absolute minimum.

This will by no means be an exhaustive description of all of the equipment possibilities for practical shooting, but it should give you some good direction. The philosophy of having a simple set of reliable gear that fits you and fits your shooting is really what you need. Endlessly chasing the latest and greatest gear is far less productive than spending your time developing better technique.

## Gear Selection

Before you get too far down the equipment rabbit hole, something needs to be made clear. There is no magic combination of gun and gear. People tend to get pretty excited about what gun they are using and love to debate what gun is best. In reality, you can do very well with almost any gun that is remotely reasonable for competition, provided you are familiar with the gun and it is fitted properly for you.

Shooters tend to be more interested in equipment than technique or training schedules. It is in many ways human nature, but that really doesn't make it helpful or productive. If you aren't sure what gear you should have, then just look at the most dominant shooters in the division you are interested in. You don't need to copy them exactly, but looking at their gear is going to give you some idea about which guns are competitive and which equipment you should consider first. You don't always need to run with the pack, but don't reinvent the wheel when there is no need. Chances are that others before you have made the mistake you may be thinking of making when it comes to gear, and you can avoid it by watching what the successful shooters are using.

From Ben:

I am, in many ways, an exception to this rule because I started my competitive shooting career with a Beretta and used one to get to a world-class skill level. Nobody else was shooting one at the time, and I endured quite a bit of ridicule using a double-action Beretta in a time where everyone was shooting striker-fired guns with heavily tuned triggers. That only worked for me because I made sure the Beretta I was using fit me properly. At that time, I believed that a heavier double-action gun was, in many ways, a better solution to the problem than the striker-fired polymer guns. I had to struggle a little bit to find proper holsters, and my life would have been easier if I had just used the same equipment everyone else was using.

## The Gun

The core of your practical shooting equipment is your gun. In many ways, the division you select is going to guide you to the best gun for you. When shooting a race gun division like Open or Limited (Standard in the rest of the world), you are likely going to choose to have a gun built to your specifications. It is imperative you do your homework and make those choices very carefully! You are going to make some expensive decisions that, in many cases, are hard to modify down the road. If you choose a 2011 with a particular style grip, you are going to spend substantial time and money fitting a new grip to the gun later if you discover you made the wrong choice.

There are some outstanding options on the market now for Production-made guns that will work for race gun divisions. CZ and Tanfoglio produce virtually the same pistols as their very nice Production guns but styled for race gun divisions in terms of trigger and caliber. As an example, if you use a CZ Shadow 2 in the Production division, the Tac Sport models from CZ are very similar, and they are set up as race guns. Perhaps they are not as nice as a custom-built gun, but they are quite a lot cheaper and easier to get, plus spare guns and parts will be more readily available.

For Production and Carry Optics (Production Optics anywhere else in the world), the options are interesting and continue to get more interesting all the time. It wasn't so long ago that people in the US were mostly shooting relatively light striker-fired guns (such as Glocks) with a few people shooting something else. Nowadays, things have shifted toward steel-framed, double-action guns along with quite a few new options for striker-fired guns. You can even get very nice polymer-framed double action guns. Basically, you can pick a light or heavy style gun (polymer for light or steel/polymer with composite for heavy) and then an action type (DA/SA or striker-fired), and you will have a few manufacturers to choose from in each given style. It's really a golden age for Production gun options now compared to just a few years ago. Rules have also been relaxed on Production gun modification, so you can tune your chosen gun specifically for your needs if you so desire.

Most people who have tried one tend to prefer a heavy pistol because it dampens the perceived recoil quite a bit. It is very true that a heavy (generally steel-frame) gun is going to feel nice and stable when it is in recoil. However, it will also be more challenging to transition with precision due to the added weight. In the end, it ends up mainly being a matter of preference and division. Shooting major power factor through an all-polymer gun is a much different consideration than shooting minor through the same gun in a different division where minor would be appropriate. The best advice is to consider the whole picture when selecting a gun and setup. A decision that seems perfect in one context may hinder you in another. It's best to try several options when possible before making an expensive decision on which gun to get. Shooting your friend's guns in practice, renting guns at ranges that have the latest models, or trying things at demo events where manufacturers provide samples is a great idea.

## Gun Fitting

Fitting your pistol to your hand is one of the least understood and most often neglected areas when it comes to selecting your handgun. It is common to see shooters with guns so small they cannot effectively grip the gun. It is also normal to see shooters with oversized magazine releases that they commonly bump and inadvertently drop the magazine from their gun while shooting. Prioritizing the right things can get you the optimal setup and avoid problems.

The number one priority for you as a shooter is that your gun is large enough for you to grip it effectively. It's a way bigger problem to have a gun with a grip that is too small for you vs. one that is too big for you. Let that sink in for a moment, since most people's natural assumption would be the opposite. That doesn't mean a gun that is too big for you to the point you can't effectively reach the trigger is going to work either, but if the grip is too small you simply will never have the level of recoil control you need to shoot effectively. Your support hand should have enough real estate so it can make contact with the grip panel on the support side. You need to be able to weld the meat of your palm into the gun and stop the gun from sliding around at all inside of your support hand. This is the primary consideration when it comes to gripping your pistol. If there isn't a solution with that gun (via replaceable back straps or grip panels) to achieve this level of contact, then I would advise picking a new gun. It's that important.

You need to be able to reach the trigger and safety without moving your hand around on the gun. To reiterate, you shouldn't need to shift your hand on the pistol so much as a millimeter to make the gun fire or to work the safety on the gun. These items should be considered nonnegotiable. If either of these items are not comfortable, then see if there is some sort of solution to modify those items. Changing the trigger or the safety can usually solve the problem on most guns. Make sure you aren't breaking equipment rules with whatever you are doing, but often there will be a solution for the issue available from the gun manufacturer or an aftermarket supplier.

It is nice to be able to reach the magazine release and the slide stop for the gun without moving around, but it isn't required. Many top-level shooters need to move their hand to reach these particular controls, and it really isn't a big problem. There are simple technique fixes, and it shouldn't be considered a big equipment problem that must be solved. Many top shooters "flip" the gun slightly in their grip to hit the magazine release, which is not uncommon and shouldn't be considered a problem.

There are occasionally issues like "riding the slide stop" that you should look out for. The Sig 226 is notorious for that issue where, for most shooters, the slide stop simply will never work because the shooter's thumb is pressed against the release when gripping the pistol normally.

A big trap some people fall into is getting a pistol that simply cannot be fitted for them, because they didn't consider fit when selecting that particular model. This means they are going to be hamstrung by something that will never work properly for them. A pistol not fitting you properly and/or not being comfortable is something that should disqualify that pistol from consideration for competition. Again, you'll want to think about these issues up front and "try before you buy" to ensure you don't make a costly mistake that will also hinder your performance.

## Backup Guns

If you are serious about shooting and you are traveling around the country for matches or classes, then you need to have a backup gun. It's smart to pick a competition gun that you can afford to buy two of. Having two identical $600 pistols is much more beneficial to your shooting than having one $1200 pistol. Most serious shooters have both a designated "match" and "practice" pistol. The "match" pistol is reserved for only shooting matches, and it should run flawlessly and be well maintained. The "practice" pistol is used for dry and live fire practice, so all the wear goes on the practice gun, and your match gun stays pristine and functioning 100 percent.

When you travel to a match or practice session, bring both your guns. At a match, you'll know you have a spare for everything because you can just remove parts from the practice gun if needed. If your match gun breaks, then you still have the practice gun. When you are doing practice, then the reverse is true. If the practice gun breaks, use the match gun for the day until you work out a solution.

## Testing Your Gun

When you get a new gun, you should test it because even the most reliable model of firearm will occasionally not work. Even the most reputable brands produce lemons from time to time. You simply can't trust a gun 100 percent until it has been adequately tested. Shooting 1,000 rounds of ammunition without cleaning or lubrication and having no failures of any sort is a good test. If your pistol does that, it should be good to go. Pistols wear over time, and things break, so a gun that is perfectly reliable one year may develop issues down the road. Testing is a continual process and you need to pay attention to any problems. Do not dismiss malfunctions as fluke events. They seldom are, there is probably an underlying problem that needs to be addressed.

Don't be shy about shooting your guns in practice to the point of failure. See how dirty they can get before they have reliability issues. How long can the springs last before they break? Do you need to apply lubrication at certain times? Pay attention to your equipment, and you'll know how to make it work and keep it working.

You should also research the model of gun you shoot to see where the weak points are. There will be areas you need to pay extra attention to on all guns, and there are certain replacement parts you would be well served to have on hand. Spending a few dollars on parts that go with you to training can save a practice session from being ruined by a broken gun.

From Joel:

When I'm at a match, I never have any doubt or worry about my gear. I bring a gun I have tested and know it's sighted in, with magazines I trust, and ammunition that I have checked carefully. My shooting performance is the only thing I need to worry about at a match. It makes the day so much more enjoyable and adds to my confidence knowing I am prepared.

## Sights

Sadly, it is a fairly common occurrence for a USPSA shooter to go to a match with a gun that isn't sighted in. Don't let that be you. The style of sight you choose is personal preference. It is easy to recommend a fiber optic front sight and a black rear sight. Some guns might have fixed or adjustable rear sights. I don't have a preference between the two, as long as the gun is sighted in and hits where I look.

Be aware the height over bore distance on red dot sighted pistols will make them hit at different places at different distances. This won't be an issue for hitting a full-size A zone but may become an issue on tight partial targets at various distances. Make sure you test your gun on close, medium, and far partials so you know how to hit any target you see in a match.

## Trigger

The trigger seems to be a main consideration that most people focus on when deciding what makes a "good" or "bad" gun. How many times has someone offered to let you hold their gun, and the first thing they tell you is to try the trigger? The main thing to look for is a trigger that has a smooth and consistent break. You don't need to have the lightest or most crisp trigger to be able to shoot the gun well.

Something you will see fairly often is someone with a trigger set so light that it compromises reliability. They might keep trying lighter and lighter springs until they find the lightest springs possible to reset the gun or ignite primers. The gun might be fine for a few thousand rounds, but after the springs set in or the gun gets a little dirty, they start getting light hits on the primers and the gun no longer fires every time they pull the trigger.

The best way to overcome this issue is not to use super light springs in your gun. Pick springs in the medium weight range that you test and know it will fire every time you pull the trigger, especially after several thousand rounds of training. You will not notice the extra weight when shooting in competition.

## Magazines

You need to make sure your magazines work by testing them thoroughly in practice. Make sure they work under all the conditions you will see in competition. Examples of this would be testing them with a round in the chamber with a completely full magazine to make sure it cycles all the way through the mag. Make sure the gun locks open after the last round fired if applicable. Check to make sure they feed reliably from slide lock as well.

Pay attention to how often your magazines need to be cleaned before they malfunction, or the follower gets stuck halfway through the mag. In a match, you should always clean your mags before they get to the point of failure, but it's nice to know where that failure point is.

If you can afford it, use separate match and practice mags, so you have pristine magazines to use in competition. An old set of match mags can be rotated out to become practice mags. Practice mags can also help identify failure points since they will wear out before the relatively fresh match mags do. Once the practice mags are worn out, they can become dry-fire mags.

## Ammunition

Most factory ammunition is reliable, but make sure you have tested your particular "lot" or batch of ammo to make sure it meets the required power factor. The lot number should be printed on the box and is a way the manufacturer groups batches of ammo. Do not assume the printed velocity on the box is the velocity it will make out of your gun. You should also shoot a fair amount of that "lot" through your gun to make sure it's reliable.

## Reloaded Ammunition

Most serious competitors reload their own ammo due to cost. It is imperative that you have a quality control system in place if you will be shooting reloaded ammo in matches. Many competitors do less quality control on their practice ammo to save time, and then make sure everything is perfect with the match ammo.

Having a gun malfunction during a match is disastrous. Make sure you use a case gauge or the barrel of your gun to verify that every round of your ammo will chamber. Any ammunition that is questionable should automatically get placed in your practice ammo bucket. If any round is clearly way out of spec, you'd be well advised to chuck it and not even use it for practice. Your match ammo should be pristine. Primer seating depth is another area you should pay special attention to. If it's possible with your particular reloading setup, your primers should be just below flush to ensure they will ignite when fired.

Make sure you are loading your ammo hot enough to give you a buffer, so you know you will still make your declared power factor even if the Chrono is reading a little light at a particular match. This point cannot be emphasized enough. There is no real performance advantage to shooting marginally light ammunition. However, if you do not meet your declared power factor at a match, you are going to have a major issue, so the risk/reward balance is clearly in favor of making sure your ammo is going to make power factor easily.

## Belt Rig

Having a proper belt rig is important since it will be holding your gear in place at competitions. You don't need the most expensive or flashy equipment, but you do need gear that is durable and works well, so it won't hold you back.

The Velcro double belt system with inner and outer belt is the most consistent setup for competition. The belt itself is rigid, so it keeps your equipment from moving around. It also keeps the orientation of everything the same, so it's easy to know where the gun or magazines will be when you need to find them quickly.

Most holsters work fine as long as they don't bind or hold the gun too tightly. Be sure to check to make sure the holster isn't interfering with any controls on the gun. Examples would be hitting the safety or bumping the magazine release if you push down on the gun in the holster. Especially if you're running an extended mag release on your gun, this can be an issue, and the result is often drawing your gun, aiming at a target, and after one shot is fired the mag falls out of the gun. There is no excuse for having this happen, check your holster closely.

The holster body attachment to the belt is also quite important. It is easy to recommend using a hanger system that holds the holster very firmly. It will give you the benefit of adjusting the height of the holster to your preference, as well as keeping it from flexing or moving during the draw. Make sure that your holster and magazine pouches are set up to comply with the equipment rules in your division. Don't let yourself be in the position of showing up at a large match after months of practice and countless hours of dry fire, just to be instructed to move your equipment.

A gear question that comes up fairly often is whether you should use bullets out or bullets forward for magazine orientation. There are people who are genuinely fast using both methods. If you are already fast with bullets forward, there probably isn't much of a reason to switch to bullets out since you would be training to try and reproduce the times you were already getting. If you find you have issues getting to the magazines consistently with bullets forward, then you might find that the mags are more accessible with bullets facing out. It's more of a consideration of comfort over speed. Use whichever is most comfortable and consistent for you and don't feel like you're "missing out" by not using the other method, they both work fine.

## Eye Protection

There are lots of options for eyewear and there isn't a "one size fits all" option. Before you overthink eyewear, you have to keep in mind that many National Championships have been won with $15 gas station sunglasses and $8 Walmart clear safety glasses. Spending money on this stuff is not going to help you all that much.

For most people, it is recommended to have at least two pairs of glasses (or swappable lenses) with you. First, you should always have a pair of clear glasses with you. It could be overcast, maybe the sun isn't up first thing, or perhaps the match has a "dark house" or a stage with a lot of shade or cover that would make the targets tough to see with sunglasses. It's also a good idea to bring a pair of sunglasses with you. The specific option for lens type (polarized, prism, etc.) is up to you, but you want something you can use for the majority of the time at the range so you get used to how things look through them, and this should be the pair you wear when you train outdoors as well.

Different lenses will make the sights appear differently, and one model might make the sights "pop" more or easier to track than other models. Hopefully, your friends have a few options to try so you can pick a favorite. Many people opt for a nice frame with a set of swappable lenses for different light conditions.

It should also be noted that if you wear corrective lenses, and don't wear contact lenses, then investing in a pair of prescription shooting glasses and/or sunglasses can be money well spent. Particularly for older shooters, vision changes may make the sights more difficult to see clearly, and having glasses set up to give you the best advantage to see what you need to can make a difference. Basically, you don't want your vision to be a limiting factor in your shooting performance.

## Hearing Protection

There are a lot of choices for hearing protection, with most of them being a type of ear plug or muff. Electronic hearing protection is excellent for awareness when not shooting, but many people recommend turning them off when it's your turn to shoot. You don't want the distraction of listening to people in the squad talking or joking as you make ready or shoot a stage. You also don't want to become reliant on any type of audible feedback you get from amplified hearing, because you might find yourself on a stage where there is too much noise around you (gunfire or people talking) to hear what you are used to hearing in practice.

Using earplugs and earmuffs at the same time is a good idea if you are sensitive to the sound, or feel that the loud noise bothers or distracts you. A prime example is anyone shooting Open division; it would be a good idea to "double plug" because it's a lot louder and you can damage your hearing if you're not careful.

## Ancillary Gear

It is wise to be prepared for any situation in a match. Most people make sure they have everything they will need with them. A better solution is to have everything you are sure to need, and then other additional items in case of an unexpected event or emergency. Taking the time to prepare some commonsense backup and service items is certainly time well spent.

Make sure you have an extra battery for your red dot with you. Bring a small screwdriver set in case something on your gear comes loose. Have a few towels with you, extra sunscreen, have snacks, and more water than you think you'll need. If the range is dusty or there's a chance of rain, have a gun cover—even a hotel shower cap would do. Have a bag to carry all that stuff in so you are organized.

Being prepared and feeling comfortable will make match day more manageable for you and give you one less thing to worry about.

Joel's Gear Test:

This is my process for making sure my match gun is ready to go, and I trust it enough to take it to a match. The exact round count doesn't really matter. The point is to have a system for testing your gear and replacing parts before they break. This is just for informational purposes.

I replace every spring in my match gun roughly once a year. The exact timing may vary, but the important thing is I replace parts before they break or become a problem. Springs are relatively cheap, and the peace of mind is worth it.

I do light cleaning after every match and check the gun over. After a full disassembly for the occasional major cleaning, I shoot the gun a minimum of 300 rounds to make sure everything was put back together correctly, and it still functions as it should.

If I have a new gun to test, or something breaks/fails and I have to replace a significant part like an extractor, I shoot the gun 1,000 to 2,000 rounds to make sure it's reliable. A new gun will likely get shot even more before I trust it. The testing starts over if I still have problems or have to replace more parts. I want to know for sure that the gun is reliable before ever using it in a match.

If a magazine starts having issues of any kind, it automatically gets moved to the training mag pile, and I will no longer use it in matches.

# CHAPTER 20
# RANGE FAMILIARIZATION

Having a feeling of being "at home" on the shooting range can have quite a dramatic effect on your performance at a match. Let me give a little example of how much this can help.

At a major match on a range that isn't familiar to you, you find yourself five shooters down in the shooting order. This is fine so far. You have walked through the stage properly and feel like you're ready to go. Unfortunately, you find yourself getting a strong desire to go to the bathroom. This isn't a minor situation you are feeling, either. Your stomach feels upset, and you are going to need to find a bathroom right now. You are pretty sure there are some portapotties around the corner from the bay you are on, and you walk over that way. The one you find is occupied, so you keep walking, looking for another. After walking past five more stages, you still don't see any. You ask around and locate a bathroom 100 yards from where you are now. You realize you might need to hurry because you were only five shooters down when you walked off, so you run a little bit to reach the bathroom and take care of your business. You can probably see where this is going now. By the time you make it back to your stage, they are calling your name as the next shooter, and you feel rushed and don't feel you had the proper walkthrough and prep time. The several minutes you spent locating a proper bathroom came back to bite you, and potentially impacted your score on the stage in a negative fashion.

The above story is something that does happen at matches, but something that people tend not to give a whole lot of thought to. Being familiar with a shooting range and with the layout and where everything is located can matter quite a lot. This is one of the things you should pay some attention to when you arrive at an unfamiliar range (hopefully) the day before you are shooting a big match.

In addition to the bathroom locations, there are a few other things you should absolutely pay attention to.

If possible, you should try to understand the layout of the range and how the stages are numbered. If the range is simple, something like 10 stages in a line numbered sequentially 1–10, then that job isn't going to be very hard. Most large ranges are not quite that easy, however. They might have one section of bays over here, and another section over there, with maybe a couple of bays off in the corner of the property, or something to that effect. Understanding the layout is going to be helpful in several ways.

First, if you know the layout of the range pretty well, you will know what stages you are shooting in what order. Especially the day before you are scheduled to shoot, you might find a particular stage complex or challenging and want to devote some additional attention to it, and you'll know exactly which stage number it is.

It is also convenient to understand the parking situation at the range so you can park your car in an advantageous spot. Often at a match, you will have an opportunity to park your vehicle near a place you will be passing in the middle of the day. In that case, you can store more ammo or beverages or whatever inside the car. You will easily be able to grab that stuff and anything else you need during the day. You should be setting yourself up to have access to the things you need throughout the day in the easiest manner possible.

The first big match I traveled to (Ben):

Very early on in my shooting career, I drove five hours or so to my first "travel" match. It was the biggest match I had ever shot in my life up to that point. It was a USPSA State Championship in a neighboring state.

When I arrived after a long car journey, I was surprised by what I saw. Everything was different! The range was different, built far differently than the local ranges I was used to. There were some spots where woods were the fall zone for bullets, there wasn't a proper berm or backstop. The walls on the stages were constructed quite differently than I was accustomed to. The walls were snow fence instead of the plastic used at the ranges at home.

It took me quite a while to really get my bearings with what I was doing. On every level, the match felt so wholly unfamiliar, and it didn't help that I didn't really know anyone there.

The strategy I used to get comfortable was to walk around the stages the day before I shot and look at the targets. No matter what the layout of the stages was like, or the construction, or the setting, or any of the other elements, the targets were familiar. Good old USPSA targets that I was very familiar with. I drilled it into my head that no matter what, the targets were the same. All I had to do was shoot.

Home field advantage is definitely a real thing. Think about the comfort level you have if an Area or Section match is held at one of your local clubs. You know where to park, you know exactly how the range is set up, and you feel more comfortable. Familiarizing yourself with the range when travelling is a way to work toward that level of comfort, which will increase each time you return to that same range.

# PART 6
# STAGE STRATEGY

# CHAPTER 21
# STAGE BREAKDOWN

There is one warning or caveat that needs to be put on the table before we get into the stage strategy discussion. A lot of the issues discussed in this section are complex. It is never as simple as "never shoot steel first" or "always enter a position on the outside target" or whatever other standard or rule you care to mention. Every decision you make has many aspects to it, and on a complicated stage, the order you decide to shoot the targets has many considerations. If you want some hard and fast rule that will carry you through every situation or scenario, you're out of luck. Our intent here is to open up your thinking and give you an approach to stage planning that will allow you to understand the stage and make good decisions for yourself.

Let's discuss the process of deciding on how to shoot a stage. Many people call this "breakdown" of stages or "walking" stages or "stage planning." It's always helpful to walk the stages the day before the match or before the match starts, if you have the option. It gives you a lay of the land if you haven't been to the range before, so you won't have to worry about getting lost on match day. It also gives you a preview of all the skills that will be tested and will help you feel more comfortable.

There will be some stages you can figure out in one minute, and stages that might take you more than ten minutes to create a solid plan for. It really depends on the match and the complexity of the stages. It's important to have a standard routine for walking stages so you can do it efficiently, without forgetting anything you should be looking at.

Gathering information about the stages, and actually deciding how you want to shoot them, should happen at a few different points. As we discussed earlier, this would include previewing stage diagrams in the weeks and days leading up to the match, and then walking the stages prior to the commencement of the match. Depending on the ruleset and the particular match, you will get varying levels of information from these processes. You should take every advantage you possibly can, to understand the stages before the match starts. When your squad gets the official stage briefing and you are working "on the clock" you don't want to still be formulating your stage plan.

## Understand the Stage

The first thing you need to do when analyzing a stage is to read the written stage briefing. That will tell you the starting position, how many targets there are, how many shots are scored per target, if extra shots are allowed, and any stipulations such as one-handed shooting. The main idea at this point is to understand what the stage is requiring of you and what skills are being tested here.

After reading the stage briefing, the first thing to do is to locate all the targets and determine what shooting position(s) they are available from. This is very often much easier said than done. Some stages have a very obvious layout where it doesn't take much work to determine where everything is. On other stages it can take substantial time and planning in order just to figure out where all the targets are, and where they can be shot from. In typical stages, expect that you will not have trouble figuring out where you can see most targets from, but a few targets will be visible from multiple spots.

If the stage is on the more complex side, sometimes it's helpful to walk behind the stage outside the shooting area. You can then stand behind a target and look back toward the shooting area. The part or parts of the stage that you see from the target are the places the target is available to be shot from. This method can help you clear things up more quickly than walking around in the shooting area looking for targets, especially if it is crowded with other people walking the stage.

There are a few common areas of concern when it comes to understanding the target location.

First and foremost, pay attention to targets that you can see from multiple spots. This is especially true in scenarios where that target looks like it is part of a set or array of targets in more than one spot. This target will tempt you into engaging it more than once, and this is something you will need to plan around.

You should take note of "hidden" targets that aren't actually hidden strictly speaking but may require an unusual or awkward position to see them. A target may only be available from a tiny sliver of the shooting area in the middle of a long stage. This is another situation you will want to plan for later on.

If there are targets that are hidden behind steel poppers, or activated by steel poppers, that is another area you will want to pay close attention to. Get clarification immediately on what targets or props activate other things, or open ports, or whatever. You can walk out on the range and follow the cables to verify which elements are activated by which targets or props if you have any questions. You need to understand that stuff right away, and you don't want to be confused.

The main thing to look for is which shooting positions you have to go to in order to see all the targets. At this phase, you probably don't want to be committing to a specific target order or even shooting position order. Understand the layout of the stage in its entirety in terms of targets and shooting positions before worrying about the actual plan.

**Choose Your Path**

At this point, you should choose your path through the stage. It is best to think of this in terms of shooting positions. You know where the targets are available from, and obviously, you need to engage each one from a predetermined shooting position. You should obviously pick a plan that puts you in a spot to engage every target. The default order for a right-handed person is to work the positions up range to downrange, left to right. Obviously, not every stage lends itself to that, but that is a general rule to get you started on figuring things out.

In addition to the "default" order, the other rule to pay attention to in terms of the selecting the order is to give yourself a chance to keep moving and shooting at the same time when it is advantageous to do so. For example, imagine a stage with three shooting positions. One of the positions has close targets that you feel comfortable shooting without stopping. The other two positions have shots you consider difficult enough that you need to stop in order to engage effectively. It is better in theory that the shooting position you don't have to stop in is shot in the middle of the stage. Obviously, you can continue moving between the hard stops if you can shoot through the targets in the middle.

You should also consider the ease of movement between positions. Imagine this common scenario. You have two shooting positions, one directly down range of the other. You are approaching these two shooting positions from somewhere else on the stage. It is easier and faster (not to mention a minimized risk of a DQ) to shoot these positions in the order of up range to downrange. Even though the distance between them is the same, you will have an easier time moving downrange than the reverse. This is one reason for the general rule of preferring to work stages (for a right-handed person) left to right, up range to downrange.

The ease of moving between positions isn't just about working your way downrange. Stages often have things you need to move around, or awkward positions you need to get into. You want to navigate through those positions in a way that allows you to finish your movement in tight or awkward spots and allows you to move through the easier parts while stopping less. If you have a choice to move forward at the end of a stage to a wide open target that can be shot on the move on the right, or a tight leaning partial target on the left, it should be obvious that it's faster to shoot the target on the right and then end on the target on the left. This would be an example of when the left-to-right preference for a right-handed shooter would be overridden based upon the actual layout of the stage.

The general term for picking your path through a stage in a way that allows more continual movement is "flow." You will often hear shooters at matches talk about how a specific stage plan "flows" for them. This is important. You really do want the movement through your plan to feel effortless and easy. You want to feel like you can keep moving on the easy stuff then really work your way into the more complicated areas.

Magazine capacity and reloading the gun shouldn't be a primary consideration at this time. Imagine your gun holds an infinite amount of ammo and try to find the fastest and most efficient way to shoot all the targets without doing anything confusing or awkward. People who let the round count and reloading requirements of their gun/division drive their stage planning are limiting themselves right off the bat, and this is a very common mistake that shooters make, particularly low-capacity division shooters. All that a lower-capacity division means for you is more reloads, and you don't need to hamstring all your thinking at this point to the number of rounds your gun holds. It should be very rare for you to alter a stage plan based upon where you need to reload. Pick your plan through the stage that is the most efficient and reload where necessary inside of that plan.

"Air gunning" the stage is something you should be doing, which is holding your hands like you'd hold your handgun and imagine shooting the targets. This gives you a good idea of how shooting the stage will feel. It also provides useful feedback for how a long lean on a stage will feel, and helps you identify any issues you might have early. You should be aware of things like the position of walls or barriers and make sure you plan to give yourself space to work around those objects without your gun banging into them.

It's important to look at all possible plans if there are multiple options. Try to keep your plan simple and avoid complicated plans that have you switching back and forth between arrays of targets. Shooting the targets in the order that you see them as you move through the stage is usually an excellent place to start for your plan.

Your preference may be to make a stage plan based on the consideration of reloading the gun being left- or right-handed. A right-handed shooter will prefer moving from left to right so the magazine well will face them, and it's easier to reload without breaking the 180. Again, and this is an idea that can't be repeated too often, a single rule or concept should not strictly dictate your stage plan. There are going to be exceptions, and you shouldn't limit yourself to options that fit a narrow rule.

Even when a stage appears symmetrical at first glance, don't trust your initial impression. There are plenty of stages where the designer tried to make it symmetrical, but they often end up a little different when built. Sometimes a wall or some other element is in a slightly different position on one side of the stage or the other, and may provide some advantage to running in a particular direction. Always take a close look at the stage and address it for what it is on the ground.

## Specific Positions

Generally speaking, the term "position" is used pretty loosely. Most stages are constructed so that standing in one spot, or standing a couple feet away in any direction, effectively makes no difference to the shooting. Like most general guidelines, this is true until it isn't. When you identify a spot on a stage that demands you stand in a very specific location, then you need to treat that position differently. Instead of a shooting position being a general spot, it becomes very specific. A common example of this would be a shooting position that requires you to lean out over a fault line. If you are standing exactly in the optimal spot for the lean, then the shooting is much easier than standing even a few inches away from the optimal spot. In this scenario, deciding on your footwork and where you'll stop for a position is just as important as the shooting. If you are even slightly mispositioned, it can make life difficult for you during the stage run.

When you identify this scenario during the stage review, you should pay close attention to it. During the walkthrough, it's important to pick the exact spot you want to stand in or shoot a target from. Using visual "markers" on a stage can be a big help for finding the exact spot when it matters. Examples are seams between two fault lines, a spot where the ground changes from grass to dirt, a wall section you want to stand next to, or any other element that stands out and is easy for you to identify. You should prioritize finding that "marker" during your walkthrough and incorporate it into your visualizations of the stage.

You should also think about the direction you want to face and how your feet should be set in each shooting position. It's important to consider how wide the transitions in that position are, and in which direction you will leave that position. Ideally, you stand "square" to the center of a group of targets you are shooting, and you should again think about those issues during your stage walk-through and visualization.

## Distance of Movement vs. Distance to Target

One very common consideration in the stage breakdown process when selecting your shooting positions is that of trading off more movement to get closer to the targets. You very often will have the option to move closer to the targets if you want to. This can be anything from moving a yard or two closer to a group of targets, to sometimes running an extra 50+ yards. This will obviously depend on how the stage is set up, but there are a few guidelines you should pay attention to.

Most of the time you will not profit from making the shooting more difficult if you are only saving a step or two. This is a very common mistake that people make, preferring to eliminate every step of movement possible, and thinking that the extra speed from moving less with pay off. A typical example of this would be stopping just before a vision barrier and leaning a little bit to see the targets. If you go a step further, you can see all the targets comfortably without the lean. This is a common situation where people are making things harder, and not saving any time doing so. You should not spend much time fussing over half a step most of the time.

The better you get at shooting, and the more speed biased the division you are shooting is, then the more likely you will profit from saving every last possible step. Open guns with compensators and dots make longer shots easier and faster, and moving up toward the targets is almost irrelevant. On the flipside, with iron sights and very risky shots with no-shoots all over the place, less risk and more reward will be had by getting closer and making the shots easier.

The best strategy is to pay attention during your training to the times and, most importantly, the hits you get on different targets at different distances. You will likely find that shooting targets from further away doesn't always add a lot of time, but you usually end up down more points. If you are paying attention to the results during your training and carefully assessing your average performance in a specific scenario, in addition to your best and worst outcomes, you should be equipped to make decisions on where you should engage targets from in a stage.

Absent specific data from training, you should take a gut check about what you feel comfortable with. If you feel like you are going to be able to shoot faster and more aggressively on a bunch of targets by taking a few extra steps, then you should listen to yourself. If you feel confident in your ability to nail longer shots and save some time, then do it. Your instincts on this tend to be correct as long as you are paying attention to it in training. Confidence is everything here, if you aren't confident you can pull something off, then it's probably a bad idea to try in a match.

## Picking the Target Order

After you select your path through the stage and have your shooting positions defined, it's time to consider the specific order you will engage the targets in. You'll have lots of options for the engagement order on target arrays or groups of targets. There will be plenty of discussion in this section about all of these nuanced strategies when it comes to picking the order of targets. However, as a general rule, you should shoot things in the order they appear and disappear, from left to right or right to left.

The alternate considerations that will tempt you can usually be nullified by you just training more and getting better. For example, a preference from most people is to shoot the "easy" targets as they come into a position. However, with training, you should be able to come into a position aggressively and nail a tight shot without too much of an issue. Just remember that getting better, or training yourself to be comfortable in all scenarios, is really the simplest solution to just about any shooting problem.

You might feel like some particular order is faster than another. However, any order that is more complicated than just working across the targets as they appear is going to add in more gun movement as well needing to remember to use a more complex order. You can lose a lot of time when transitioning the gun more than needed in a zig-zag pattern. The time lost in the zig-zagging generally offsets anything gained by the "faster" engagement order.

Sometimes you can profit from an unusual target engagement order, such as when you can group like targets together to make less work for yourself. For example, if you have a mix of close-range paper targets along with distant steel targets all jumbled up in front of you, you might feel more comfortable engaging the paper first, then the steel. A common situation you might see is a couple of close paper targets (let's say you shoot them left to right), with a transition out onto a group of distant steel plates between the paper targets, that you can engage (working back from right to left). This is easier for many people because you will attack the paper targets essentially looking through the gun, and then shoot the steel in "sniper" mode carefully pressing the trigger for each shot. If you shoot the close paper targets first, then the steel, you only need to change "modes" one time on that set of targets instead of multiple times if all of the targets were engaged left-to-right.

## Choose Your Aim Points

As you are assessing the targets on the stage, you should carefully select an "aim point" on each target. This usually means you are going to aim at the center of the A zone on paper or the center of the calibration circle of a popper. It is extremely productive to actually look at the exact point you wish to hit during your stage walkthrough, as this increases your accuracy substantially.

You will not always want to aim at the center of the target. In cases where you have a partial target, make a note to aim away from the no-shoot or hardcover a little bit to reduce the risk. Where to aim exactly depends on your division and whether or not you are scoring major or minor. This is where experimentation on the practice range really helps. Absent specific experimentation, a good rule of thumb is to aim at the center of the available target area.

You should also give some conscious thought to what your sights need to look like for a given target as well as what your trigger control precision should be. This text isn't intended to be a shooting technique manual, addressing all of the specifics of how to aim at and hit your target would take up an entire separate book. The important thing during the stage walkthrough is for you to recall your previous training, and actually think about the specific sight picture on each target that is going to work the best for you, as well as how careful you need to be with the trigger. You should visualize these elements and burn them into your stage plan.

### Shooting on the Move

Opportunities to shoot targets on the move can save a lot of time, but also add difficulty. Some people seem to always want to shoot without moving because they believe that they just can't hit the targets while moving. If they haven't practiced doing so, then they are probably right. Other people shoot on the move whenever they feel they can, even if it doesn't offer a tangible benefit. Always be mindful of risk versus reward, and make sure shooting on the move has a benefit, otherwise it just ads risk for no benefit.

The most common way to shoot while moving is shooting into and out of positions. Commonly, people will shoot a close or easy target as they are entering a position while getting set up to shoot more challenging targets from that position. Someone might shoot easy targets as they exit a position and start moving toward the next one.

A common mistake when it comes to deciding to shoot into a position is that the shooter forces the issue of shooting while moving into a place that it doesn't offer any actual advantage. Many people have an idea in their head that it is always faster to shoot while moving, and that just isn't true. It is often quicker to shoot while moving, that much is true. However, if you slow your movement speed down four or five steps from a shooting position in order to "shoot while you move" into that position, then you are not likely saving any time overall. You should shoot and move aggressively through a stage, and only shoot on the move in the places where you can do so without slowing your movement speed down to a crawl.

With training, you will learn your capabilities and limitations on shooting while moving. The easiest way to know how to actually apply your skills when it comes to this often-crucial decision to shoot on the move in a match, is to take a quick "gut check" of how you feel about a group of targets. Based upon your training experience, do you feel like you can aggressively attack that set of targets while you move or not? If there is any doubt, you are likely better off standing still.

## Magazine Capacity

Now that you know where you want to shoot everything from, and in what order, you just need to plan your reloads into it, not the reverse. It was mentioned earlier, and I'll say that again: you should not decide your target engagement plan based upon your reloads. It is intentional that the magazine capacity and reload issue isn't really considered before this point in the planning process. So many people walk through a stage and start counting out shots in order to "figure out their reloads" first thing as they assess the stage. This tends to close them off to other possibilities, or get them sucked into plans that don't really flow through the stage.

The easiest method is to pick the path and target order through the stage, and then start worrying about the reloads. Are there convenient points to reload on the stage? The more movement distance you have to get the reload in, the better in terms of speed. How many reloads will you need to do? For example, on a 32-round stage shooting a 10-round gun, you must reload at least 3 times. It doesn't matter if you shoot 2-10-10-10 or 8-8-8-8. You are going to reload at least three times on that stage. Figure out the convenient points to reload and that will make things the easiest.

The importance of prioritizing reloading while moving between positions is something lots of people overlook, particularly if they're looking for a "count" of shots to determine when to reload. For stages with longer movement between positions, you need to prioritize running as hard as you can and just get the reload done somewhere between the positions. An example would be, after you shoot the last shot in a position, your focus shifts toward running as hard as you possibly can as you exit the position. Somewhere between positions, you'll hit the mag release, grab a new magazine, and get the magazine seated so you'll be ready to get the gun up early as you enter the next position.

Without a doubt, you will run into occasions where you have a "tight" reload. This means a reload with minimal movement or maybe even no movement at all (a standing reload). This is something that you want to avoid whenever possible, but sometimes the conditions dictate it must happen. For example, if there are 18 rounds you want to fire from basically one position, and you are shooting a 15-round gun, then no matter what you do, you are going to end up having a tight reload. In this scenario, it is best just to accept that everyone in your division is going to need to eat that reload and not worry too much about it. The last thing you want to do is some silly stage plan that complicates every other part of the stage to try to mitigate that one tight reload. Very commonly, you see people shooting targets from a crazy distance or adding in a position in order to avoid the tight reloads, and that is the sort of thinking you want to avoid. Don't fear the tight reload that you can't get out of.

When you should pay attention to a tight reload is when you can get rid of it by making an extra reload in a spot that is much more convenient. A properly trained shooter should be able to reload as they run with very little time lost. That being the case, it is better to reload on the run twice rather than do a single tight reload where you are losing time. So often, people only want to do the minimum reload count to the exclusion of any other consideration, and that just doesn't make sense.

If you are a Production or Single-Stack shooter, you may have just read that section and realized that you have spent your entire shooting career planning your stages primarily around your reloads, and prioritizing shooting as many rounds from every mag over all else. Challenge yourself to eliminate this thinking and start working on stage flow and the other movement priorities going forward, and place reload considerations toward the bottom of the list.

# CHAPTER 22
# HIT FACTORS

If you are a more advanced shooter, you are likely to make a stage plan based on what you think the hit factor will be. Before we go too far down this rabbit hole, understand up front that the best strategy for most people is to shoot A's and close C's as fast as they can, without worrying about the hit factor. Doing hit factor math before you shoot the stage isn't helpful for about 90 percent of competitors. The reason this won't help most people is that they lack the training foundation to make the necessary fine adjustments to their shooting style in a match. A shooter who doesn't have the proper training is likely to shoot misses and eat no-shoots when they decide to push on a high hit factor stage. The same shooter will often slow down excessively on a stage they consider low hit factor. If you aren't sure that you can fine-tune your shooting in the middle of a match in the ways that are described in this section, then don't attempt it without putting in some time on the training range.

First, we will discuss the reason for estimating the hit factor of a stage, and then we can move on to how to make that estimation.

If the hit factor is higher on a stage, then the stage will reward speed a little bit more than it rewards accuracy.

This speed bias means that certain situations should be handled differently to support shooting faster. The reverse is always true; points are more heavily weighted on a low factor stage. This means certain scenarios should be treated differently to support shooting more points.

An excellent example to illustrate this would be a long-range target on a high hit factor stage. It takes considerable time to aim at a distant target (the definition of "considerable" and "distant" depend on your skills). In the context of a high factor stage, you are usually better off risking more points down on that distant target than spending time stabilizing the gun perfectly for each shot and giving yourself a higher probability of more A's. When you are scoring minor, you only lose four points if you shoot two more C's on a stage. You might well spend an extra second trying to get the A's when the target is at 30 yards. If the hit factor climbs up high enough, that becomes an unattractive proposition. You can then work into your planning a looser and quicker aiming style for that target.

The reverse scenario can also happen. If you have a low hit factor stage with primarily long/tight shots, then the close-range targets that are relatively easy to get A's on become targets you don't want to eat points down on.

Doing the math on the prior example, let's say it's certain that if you spend the extra one second you will get four A's and if you don't take the extra time you're guaranteed to get two A's and two C's, which drops four points shooting minor. If the hit factor on the stage is over 4.0, then it wouldn't make sense to spend the extra second getting the A's—the lower time overrides the lost points. Essentially, hit factor is "points per second" so if you can draw conclusions that a certain action will take a certain amount of time and will result in certain points changes, this can inform your decision. In reality, it's not that easy because you're dealing with PROBABILITIES of things happening, not certainties, based upon your own training and self-assessment of what you can pull off. But that is at least the math basis for what you're trying to decide.

A 4.0 hit factor stage is four points per second, and a 10.0 hit factor stage is ten points per second. You only need to make more than four additional points in a second to justify taking the extra time on the 4.0 hit factor stage, but you'd need to make over ten points additional in the 10.0 hit factor stage. So, you can see how accuracy is stressed more in the 4.0 hit factor stage and taking a little extra time to get more points is more likely to be worthwhile than the 10.0 hit factor stage. Thinking of it on the flip side: On the 10.0 hit factor stage, if you can drop a full second from your time through a more risky target engagement that is likely to lead to a few more C's, it's likely to be worth it to shoot it faster and possibly give up the points. If, for your skill level, shooting faster likely means Deltas and Mikes, then obviously this doesn't apply, which is why we mentioned up front that this concept really only applies for advanced shooters.

Doing the hit factor math might also influence your strategy on a stage that offers the option to shoot while moving. If the targets are at the edge of your comfort zone and the hit factor is low, then maybe you should stand still and get the points. If the hit factor is high, perhaps you should shoot while you move and accept some more points down.

As you can probably figure out, the application for hit factor math in your planning is relatively broad. If you are on the fence about one option vs. another, the hit factor you estimate for the stage can help you decide what the correct path is. That's really a good way to think about it: hit factor consideration of the stage is more of a minor tweak to your plan on a stage, not a primary deciding factor, so don't get too caught up in it.

|  | BASE SCORE HITS/ TIME=HF | 75% A 25%C | 75% A 25% c -2 SECONDS | 50%A 50% C | 50% A 50% c -2 SECONDS | 25% A 75% C | 25% A 75% C -2 SECONDS |
|---|---|---|---|---|---|---|---|
| MAJOR | A: 32 C: 0  TIME: 19.30  HF: 8.2902 | A: 24 C: 8  TIME: 19.30  HF: 7.8756 | A: 24 C: 8  TIME: 17.30  HF: 8.7861 | A: 16 C: 16  TIME: 19.30  HF: 7.4611 | A: 16 C: 16  TIME: 17.30  HF: 8.3237 | A: 8 C: 24  TIME: 19.30  HF: 7.0466 | A: 8 C: 24  TIME: 17.30  HF: 7.8613 |
| MINOR | A: 32 C: 0  TIME: 19.30  HF: 8.2902 | A: 24 C: 8  TIME: 19.30  HF: 7.4611 | A: 24 C: 8  TIME: 17.30  HF: 8.3237 | A: 16 C: 16  TIME: 19.30  HF: 6.6321 | A: 16 C: 16  TIME: 17.30  HF: 7.3988 | A: 8 C: 24  TIME: 19.30  HF: 5.8031 | A: 8 C: 24  TIME: 17.30  HF: 6.4740 |

*Figure 7: An example of HF with Major vs. Minor scoring.*
*This example shows how going two seconds faster affects the outcome of the hit factor when a percent of points are dropped.*

## Estimating Hit Factor

Let's move on to estimating the hit factor. You should already know the hit factor is figured by taking the points earned and dividing it by the time. The number represents how many points are being scored per second. The high hit factor wins the stage, and the other stage scores are weighted against the winning score. That part is Practical Shooting Scoring 101.

Estimating your hit factor before you shoot the stage isn't as simple as that. This requires a working knowledge of how actual scores are determined and the scores you shoot in certain scenarios. If you have never shot and scored drills on a practice range, you won't know what kind of scores to expect.

It can be easier to figure this out on USPSA Classifiers or any of a plethora of standardized drills that competitors regularly shoot. The specific exercises are outside the scope of this text, but you have almost certainly heard of them, if not shot them. Things like El Presidente and the Bill Drill are common ones. The point is that if you shot an El Presidente one time at a match, that is a different level of working knowledge than someone who has shot it multiple times in a training session. The best situation is to have shot it multiple times over countless training sessions spanning over months or years. If you know your average score, your best score, your cold score, and so forth, then you are well equipped to start estimating your hit factor on scenarios that look like that drill. Once you have shot a lot of drills and stages and developed that working knowledge, then you will be well prepared to estimate your hit factor on stages.

As a general rule, the more shooting you have without non-shooting events (such as movement) then, the higher the hit factor is going to be. The hard part for people to understand is that the hit factor isn't just determined by what the targets look like and how you shot them, but on how much other stuff you need to do on the stage. If you have two shooting positions with some targets in each position and the positions are 10 yards apart, then you can come up with some average hit factor for that stage. If you move the positions 10 yards further apart, then the hit factor will drop considerably without any other piece of the shooting problem really changing. You just end up spending more time running.

In any event, if this sounds attractive to you, then you need to develop a working knowledge of hit factors to assist your decision making on stages.

# CHAPTER 23

# MINIMIZING RISK

A nother thing to consider toward the end of your planning process is the risk level of your stage plan. There will always be an element of risk of mistakes during competition. If you shoot so slowly and conservatively that you never make mistakes, then you quite simply will never win anything. The sport is fast, and the top shooters are extremely fast. If you are chasing them, mistakes are going to happen, and trying to shoot with zero risk means you are ensuring you will never be at the top. Knowing that, adjusting your stage plan to mitigate the risk level without a major negative impact on time is something you should consider.

The most significant part of minimizing risk is knowing your skill level and being realistic about what will and could happen during a stage. This knowledge of yourself and your skills comes from practice. As you practice more and shoot more matches, you can rely on past experiences to gain a reasonable estimation of how things will go. You want to get to the point that you can look at a stage and know what you can and can't do, and what areas could be potentially risky for you.

A good example of this is a 20-yard headbox that you have the option to move up to 10 yards to engage instead. Shooting iron sights, it can confidently be said that 95 percent of shooters in USPSA cannot reliably hit a headbox on a USPSA target at 20 yards. They can't hit it shooting quickly. They can't hit it with no time limit. They cannot reliably hit it at all. Despite this, many competitors in USPSA would still choose to shoot that target farther away if they thought it would save some time. This demonstrates that many people fundamentally lack the ability to think about what is likely to happen on the stage and plan around it. They are likely operating with an unrealistic and optimistic view of what they are capable of. You don't want that to be you. Know your capabilities and make a realistic plan to shoot at your skill level while minimizing the risk.

| | BASE SCORE HITS/TIME/HF | BASE SCORE / w MISS | MISS ADJ TIME |
|---|---|---|---|
| MAJOR | A: 32<br>C: 0<br><br>TIME: 19.30<br><br>HF: 8.2902 | A: 31<br>C: 0<br>M: 1<br><br>TIME: 19.30<br><br>HF: 7.5130 | A: 31<br>C: 0<br>M: 1<br><br>*TIME: 17.49*<br><br>HF: 8.2905 |
| MINOR | A: 32<br>C: 0<br><br>TIME: 19.30<br><br>HF: 8.2902 | A: 31<br>C: 0<br>M: 1<br><br>TIME: 19.30<br><br>HF: 7.5130 | A: 31<br>C: 0<br>M: 1<br><br>TIME: 19.30<br><br>HF: 8.2905 |

*Adjusted time is to reach near base HF*

*Figure 8: This figure shows an example of the time you would have to achieve to negate a miss for Major and Minor power factor.*

| | BASE SCORE HITS/ TIME/HF | BASE /w NS & MAKE UP | BASE /w NS & MAKE UP ADJ TIME | BASE /w MISS & NS | BASE /w MISS & NS ADJ TIME |
|---|---|---|---|---|---|
| MAJOR | A: 32<br>C: 0<br><br>TIME:<br>19.30<br><br>HF: 8.2902 | A: 32<br>C: 0<br>NS: 1<br><br>TIME:<br>19.30<br><br>HF: 7.7720 | A: 32<br>C: 0<br>NS: 1<br><br>*TIME:<br>18.09*<br><br>HF: 8.2919 | A: 31<br>C: 0<br>M: 1<br>NS: 1<br><br>TIME:<br>19.30<br><br>HF: 6.9948 | A: 31<br>C: 0<br>M: 1<br>NS: 1<br><br>*TIME:<br>16.28*<br><br>HF: 8.2924 |
| MINOR | A: 32<br>C: 0<br><br>TIME:<br>19.30<br><br>HF: 8.2902 | A: 32<br>C: 0<br>NS: 1<br><br>TIME:<br>19.30<br><br>HF: 7.7720 | A: 32<br>C: 0<br>NS: 1<br><br>*TIME:<br>18.09*<br><br>HF: 8.2919 | A: 31<br>C: 0<br>M: 1<br>NS: 1<br><br>TIME:<br>19.30<br><br>HF: 6.9948 | A: 31<br>C: 0<br>M: 1<br>NS: 1<br><br>*TIME:<br>16.28*<br><br>HF: 8.2924 |

*Adjusted time is to reach near base HF*

*Figure 9: This figure shows the correlation between taking a make-up or the time you would have to achieve to negate the no shoot or miss for Major and Minor power factor.*

Be mindful of what will likely happen and if you think you'll need make-up shots. If there are eight mini poppers at 20 yards and your gun holds 10 + 1, there might be a good chance you'll need to do a slide lock reload. You should anticipate that as you create your stage plan, knowing that it could happen. Should you choose a more conservative aiming strategy for those targets? Yes, you should.

Pay attention to the pattern of the pasters on paper targets from prior shooters. If you see that a no-shoot target has been getting hit a lot, it should get your attention. Why are people hitting that no-shoot? Are you likely to do the same? Is there something you can do differently with your plan to avoid that?

In any event, pay attention to the risk level of what you are going to attempt on a stage. You should virtually never be ok eating misses or no-shoot hits. If you see elements of your stage plan that are reasonably likely to generate those results for you, knowing your own skill level and how you've shot stages in the past, then try to alter the plan to minimize the risk. "Crashing" on a stage where you have a complete disaster of penalties and/or extra time added by mistakes you are making is a scenario you absolutely want to avoid. You can't win a match with one stage performance, but you can certainly lose a match that way.

# CHAPTER 24
# ACTIVATED TARGETS

"Activated" targets are targets that get triggered to do something by some other device. Usually, they are moving targets like "swingers" that get activated by shooting down a steel target. Sometimes they are targets activated by a "stomp box" that you step on to activate. In some cases, a target doesn't move, but something else moves out of the way, exposing the target and allowing you to engage it. The possibilities are limited only to the stage designer's imagination. You should have a working knowledge of the standard stuff and also be prepared for anything that gets thrown at you.

Lots of people are afraid of activated targets or commonly have misses on them. Shooting mechanics seem to completely go out the window as the person sprays bullets at a swinging target hoping they get two hits on it. Often the primary consideration in their mind is time and not hits. A less experienced shooter might have zero confidence in their ability to hit the target, so they just spray a few bullets and move on, hoping they may have hit the target. That isn't really the best solution to the problem, and it would be better to handle those targets in a more systematic way.

There are essentially two main pieces to an activator target. First, there is shooting the target itself. This is not really an easy thing to do because, generally, the target is moving, and it moves in a predetermined way. You need to have a plan to shoot it that takes into account how it is going to move. Then there is the sequence of the targets. You often activate a moving target and then have time to complete other tasks (usually, that means shooting a different target), and then engage the activated target. This means you need to have a sequence that takes into account how quickly you complete certain tasks and how the target will be moving during that time. You only get one chance to get this right because, in a match, you shoot each stage only once. This means this stuff can get complicated quite quickly.

The target sequence is a good place to start. It seems like the top shooters always know exactly where the activated target is going to be and know exactly how much time they have to shoot things in between. That skill comes from being able to look at a target and know exactly how long each skill will take to complete. This is yet another skill that comes from regular training. The same as estimating your hit factor on a stage, if you have a working knowledge of target transition and split times for different scenarios, then you are well equipped to estimate how long various actions will take.

In the event you do not know how long things take, your best bet is to pay attention to someone of a similar skill level to yourself. By observing other shooters' attempts at a stage with a moving target on it, you get a good sense of the timing of that stage and how things will work out for you. This is the most common method for figuring these things out in a match. Obviously, if you need to shoot a stage first, this method won't be possible. It is better to know what will happen through your training, but absent that knowledge, copying other people of your level will do just fine in most cases.

Be aware that you may have things in the activator sequence other than shooting. You may have to move from one spot to another. You may need to reload. You may manipulate some other prop. It isn't always about shooting something while a mover comes out. Be aware of this possibly and don't close yourself off to the idea of doing something unconventional while the targets are moving.

When you get the official stage briefing you will see all the moving targets demonstrated for you. Watch this very carefully! You will see the mechanism for the activation. You will see the way the target moves. You will see how fast the target moves. All of these things are critical to take note of. It is not a bad idea to take a video of this so you can see it again if you like. If you have time to check out activators the day before you shoot by watching a staff pre-match or other squads shooting the day or session before you, this process can become far less stressful.

Be aware that the demonstration you see can be a little off from reality during the stage. For example, the activation speed of the target you see demonstrated may not be correct. Often the range officer will throw an activating popper down on the ground quite hard . . . much harder than a shot would. This makes the activation happen sooner than it otherwise would. The opposite can also occur. Pay attention to these things, so you don't have flawed expectations of what you will see while shooting the stage.

Once you watch the stage crew activate a target and decide on the order of engagement (whether you will be engaging other targets in between for timing purposes), stop watching targets that are momentum driven such as swingers or bobbers. These slow down with time, and often do so rapidly. Observing these targets once they are slowed down will no longer be realistic for the speed you are likely to engage them at when they are first activated.

If pulling a rope, door, handle, or another prop is the method of activation, try to get a sense of what that is going to feel like during the walkthrough. You probably won't get to pull on the activator yourself while it is set, so watch carefully while it is demonstrated. Is there a door that seems super heavy to open? Does the activator rope pull easily? Gather as much information as you can during the demonstration.

After you understand the target and its method of activation, make a plan to shoot the target. Swinging targets dwell at specific points. Targets that bob up and down obviously should be engaged when they expose themselves. The possibilities are endless. What you need to do (again) is assess the target for what it is and plan to engage it based on your own skills.

The main consideration when it comes to most moving targets is "how many shots per pass." Each time the target exposes itself to you is a "pass." Obviously the more slowly the target moves the more shots you can fire in a pass. Slow targets get the standard two shots. Faster targets typically only get one per pass. If you decide the target is quick or risky, you may choose to fire a "safety" shot, which is an extra shot that you don't strictly need, but it helps ensure you get the required hits. This is a legitimate tactic that can be employed on extremely risky targets.

One point that can't be stressed enough is that you should shoot moving targets and the associated sequences with a deliberate and careful plan. You should not "go fast" or "rush" or "spray bullets" or any of that. It is very common to see poor scores and mistakes from shooters who give up on planning and just spray bullets while they hope for the best. That isn't a very reliable strategy, and you should avoid it.

## Swingers/Bobbers

There are two main methods to shoot swingers, ambushing and tracking. Ambushing is the method you need to use if the main arc of the swinger is hidden, and you only see it appear for just a small section of its path. The only option you have is to hold the gun where you know the target will be and fire when the target comes into view. In some cases, you'll get to see the dwell where the target is slowing down and reversing direction; on others you'll need to start pressing the trigger as soon as you see the edge of the target.

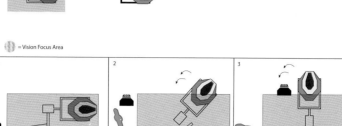

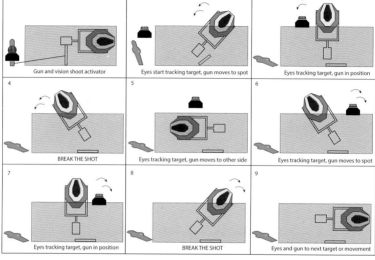

*Figure 10: Ambushing a swinger due to main arc of swinger hidden, one shot per pass: 1) Vision and Gun on activator. 2) Eyes start to track target and gun moves to spot. 3) Eyes tracking and gun in position. 4) "Break the shot." 5) Eyes continue to track target, gun to other side. 6) Eyes track target and gun moves to spot. 7) Eyes tracking target and gun in position. 8) "Break the shot." 9) Eyes and gun onto the next target or movement.*

For tracking a target when you can see a good portion of its travel, you keep your gun moving with the target as you fire the shots, even tracking it through the wall if needed. Stopping the gun when you shoot will typically result in shooting behind the target. There might be times when you can only shoot one shot per pass due to a limited exposure on a fast target. Remember, the target is going at the same speed for everyone. If you're uncomfortable shooting it twice on one pass, the other people at your skill level will be also.

= Vision Focus Area

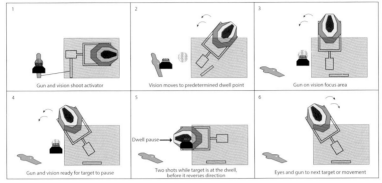

*Figure 11: Taking a swinger at the dwell: 1) Vision and gun shoot activator. 2) Vision moves to the predetermined dwell spot. 3) Gun on the vision focus area. 4) Gun and vison ready for shot. 5) Shoot possible number of shots while the target is at the dwell as there will be a slight pause before the target reverses direction (two shots in this example, may be less depending on speed). 6) Eyes and gun onto the next target or movement.*

## Max Trap/Clamshell

Some targets don't really move so much as they expose themselves for a limited amount of time. These targets have different names and methods of activation. The main theme is that you will be presented with a target for a very limited window of time, and then a penalty target will cover most of the target after the activation is complete. This would be what is referred to as a "non disappearing" target; it's fully or mostly visible during the activation, and afterward only a small portion of the target is still visible, such as just the head box. Generally, the shot you are left with if you don't shoot the target during the exposure window is extremely tight and risky, so in most cases shooting the target during activation is the preferred strategy.

These targets are almost entirely dependent on sequencing. If you get the timing right, you should be engaging the "shoot" target just as it is exposing, and you should be able to engage it without an issue.

The main thing to watch out for on these targets is being late to engage them. If you engage the target late, then the no-shoot cover target will be closing up, and you can end up inadvertently hitting it. This is obviously really bad. Consider offsetting your aim point away from where the no-shoot will be appearing from to give yourself a little more time on this target. You should also be sure not to have tunnel vision on the target you are shooting so you remain aware of the position of the no-shoot during your engagement sequence.

## Disappearing Targets

Some targets are scored as "disappearing" targets, which means that you will not be penalized for missing the target. As a general rule, you are not required to fire any shots at the target. Depending on the specific ruleset you are shooting under at the match, that may not always be the case, but it usually is.

Disappearing targets just add another decision to your stage planning. "Should I shoot at this target?" is the question you need to ask yourself. Generally speaking, it is a good idea to shoot at every target and try to get as many points as you can. However, sometimes there are exceptions to this. These targets are often a sucker's bet. If you can estimate your hit factor on stages and are able to adequately estimate timing when it comes to target sequencing, then you should be able to figure out if it is worth it to shoot these targets or not. Absent that, following what the rest of the shooters do is a good bet.

## Memory Stages

Memory stages could be loosely defined as a stage where the challenge comes more from figuring out and remembering the target and position sequence than it does from the actual shooting mechanics. When looking at a stage, if the shots don't seem to be very challenging, but the complexity of the stage layout takes some time to wrap your head around, you know you're dealing with a memory stage. It would be best if you immediately recognized that there is a risk of forgetting targets, forgetting positions, double-engaging targets, or getting confused and making some other costly mistake. These stages demand your attention and some special treatment.

You should almost certainly double-check the count of the targets and the availability of the targets. Double-checking your work and then conferring with someone else is a good way to make sure you saw everything, and you counted everything accurately. If you aren't sure, check with a third person. It may take twenty minutes to figure out how you want to run a complex memory stage, so don't be shy about getting a little help from your friends.

You may also want to work as a team to determine the layout. This is common practice at USPSA matches on complicated stages. One person stands inside the shooting area and another person on the outside, confirming the positioning and availability of targets.

You would be well advised to bias your plan more toward something that is intuitive and easy for you to remember over the theoretical fastest plan. You want to be sure you are avoiding a disaster on these stages. You don't need to win the stage to win the match. Just give the stage extra care and attention during the planning phase.

When it comes to visualization, make sure you take a few extra visualization passes before you step up to shoot. You want to confirm you are going to have zero hesitation during your run.

Finally, it isn't a bad idea to watch other people shoot the stage. If you see someone shooting from a position or at an angle that you don't plan to, then you may have made a serious mistake during your look at the stage. Double-check your work and confirm you understand the stage properly.

## Fear The DQ

Pay attention to the safety rules while you do your walk-through of a stage and pay attention to the stage briefing from the Range Officers. It is common practice for them to issue a special warning in certain places within a stage where there have been disqualifications issued for safety violations. You don't want that to be you, so pay attention.

If you see anything on the stage that you aren't sure about, ask. You want to know if you are allowed to shoot targets from positions that look borderline. You want to know where the Range Officers are calling the safe angle if there is any doubt. You may get pushback from the RO if you ask for clarification on something. Sometimes they will not (for whatever reason) want to answer questions like this directly. Take that as a cue that the borderline situation you see is likely a problem and make sure your plan is safe.

Be very mindful of where the 180-degree plane is while you're doing your walkthrough and be cautious of anywhere you could be disqualified due to breaking it. Examples would be shooting a target close to the 180 and breaking your grip as you start to reload the gun, which could cause your muzzle to go past the 180. A way to plan for this would be to program in during your walkthrough that you want to turn your upper body downrange before you start the reload.

Reloading while running toward your weak side, and running up range while reloading, are additional elements to be cautious of. Plan those movements into your stage plan and be very mindful of where your muzzle will be as you run. There might be times when it's smarter to delay the reload until you navigate around a wall, prop, or have your body turned, so you're facing downrange again.

# CHAPTER 25

# "GET BACK ON YOUR PLAN"

Your mental preparation before a stage provides your guide for what to do during the stage. You want to make a plan that you can follow without any thinking and stick with it no matter what happens. If something unexpected occurs, you don't want to have to completely alter your entire stage plan on the fly, you want to stick with your plan and adjust immediately to get back on it. A good example of this is an unplanned reload. Should your gun run out of ammunition when you don't plan to (for whatever reason), and you execute a reload, then you shouldn't change anything about your plan. Even if you reload and fire only a single round and then move again, if your plan was to reload when you begin that movement, you should reload when you start the movement. Don't think about it, just do it.

Competitors often have something go sideways with their plan, and then they never get back on it. They try to work out a new plan while they are actively shooting a stage. This isn't practical and usually compounds an already bad situation. It is common to see someone have an unplanned standing reload, and then have two more unplanned standing reloads on the same stage, as a result of never getting back on their planned reload schedule.

It is the mark of an experienced shooter when you see something catastrophic happen on a stage, and then they finish the stage normally. If you only saw the second part of their attempt at a stage, you would think that everything had happened normally. Correction of the situation and then getting back on your plan is the best thing you can do when things go wrong. Your stage plan isn't a wish list, it is a mental program for what you are going to do when you run the stage.

## Contingency Planning

This may seem like contradictory advice to what preceded it, but it is a reality that sometimes you need a "contingency plan." This sort of a plan is an "if this, then this" sort of plan. These sorts of plans are risky, and should be made cautiously. Having conscious decision making as part of a preprogrammed routine is something that is hard to do and requires everything else about your shooting to be completely automatic. However, it can be advantageous for an experienced shooter to have such a plan in certain situations.

For example, if there is a shooting position that runs the gun to capacity, but one of the targets is available again later in the stage, it might be a good idea to have the plan "If I miss this piece of steel here, I will pick it up from over there." This would allow you to avoid a standing reload in the event of missing that target with your first shot at it. This plan demands that essentially you visualize both possibilities and then process what is actually happening and make the decision on the fly to re-engage the target later on if needed.

You could have a contingency plan for many different circumstances, that is just a typical example. Again, this is a difficult thing to pull off flawlessly, and is for experienced shooters who have the rest of their technique down.

### Visualize Doing It Right

As you walk through stages and visualize what you are going to do, be aware of one essential fact: you are going to do as you visualize. The way you rehearse going through a stage is the way you are going to shoot that stage. As mentioned earlier, the mind is a powerful tool and engaging it with visualization allows a program to be run without conscious thought, which can be both good and bad.

Have you ever seen someone talk about how they need to remember "not to reload there" or something like that? You then see the person make exactly the error they were verbally telling themselves not to? This shows you the power of a mental stage rehearsal. This shooter burned the image in their mind of that spot equating to a reload, and so when they hit the spot, their body executed the reload automatically.

Often, people catch themselves doing something during the rehearsal and visualization that they do not wish to do on their stage run, and then do not correct the problem with repeated visualization passes doing it correctly. If you find yourself in this situation, it's critical to visualize exactly how you WANT to shoot the stage and visualize only that outcome. Pay attention to what is happening. You will do as you rehearse and visualize for better or worse.

**Simple. Repeatable. Aggression.**

It is important to highlight a crucial idea at the end of a section that will leave many readers with a lot of questions and challenge many things they may have believed in the past.

When you are planning stages, the most important thing is that you have something that you can attack. You need to shoot your plan with aggression. You want it to be simple enough that you go at it without thinking about it. There is no time to think. The stage is something you should be working through at the limit of your technique and skill, nothing more, nothing less. If you feel tentative and uncertain about the plan, then it's a bad plan that is too complicated. You should be confident and ready to attack the stage with your plan.

Stages can be as complicated as you want to make them. The reality is the more simply you can view the stage, the better you are going to do.

# PART 7
# SHOOTING
# A STAGE

# CHAPTER 26
# SHOOTING A STAGE

From Ben:

On the road to winning my first State-level match (an IDPA match) when I was a very new competitive shooter, I was doing great. I had been shooting for three months and doing quite well in IDPA. I wasn't super quick, but I dropped very few points. I was doing well at the State Match, and from what information I could gather, I was in the running to win the match overall.

With only a few stages left for me, there was a disaster. I had a bad malfunction in the middle of a stage. I had a round not go into the chamber. I was using factory ammunition, and a Beretta that had, up to that point, worked flawlessly. I had never had a malfunction in a match . . . let alone the nightmare I was looking at. The gun was completely locked up. A deformed round had not chambered, and I couldn't rack it out either. It was stuck.

I looked around and decided to use the structure I was in as a tool to get the gun opened. I slammed the muzzle of my gun into some wood as hard as I could. Sure enough, I was back in business right after that. The malfunction had cost me huge amounts of time . . . probably ten seconds. It was awful.

I was crushed. The match had been good up to that point, and now I would be hurt badly by this malfunction. After collecting myself by taking a minute alone and swearing at my ammo, I realized the only strategy left was to finish the match without having any more problems and let the cards fall where they may. This wasn't an easy thing for me to do at that age, but I pulled myself together and won the match in spite of the problem.

The trick that helped me get back on track was to think about how nobody else was having a perfect day. Looking around at just my squad and the other good shooters in the match, I could hear everyone talking about this mistake or that issue. It was constant. I knew that a bad malfunction was going to hurt me, but if that was the worst I had that day, I would still be in a position to possibly win. That little bit of perspective helped me a whole lot.

The ideal outcome when you shoot a stage is that you execute the stage to the full ability you have trained yourself to possess.

If you sit back and think about that for a minute, you should realize that when it comes to actually shooting a stage in a match, there is nothing you are going to be able to do better than execute at your trained ability. Sure, there are certainly quite a few things you can do to maximize your performance, but no matter what you do you are capped out at your trained ability.

Another way of thinking about this concept is that most people in a sterile environment will just walk up to the stage or challenge and shoot it to their ability. What I mean by a "sterile environment" is a place that is free from competitive or social pressure. Think about what happens on your training range when you are by your-self, generally you set up your drill or exercise and do your thing. You aren't worried a lot about what anyone else would think about what you are doing, you are just shooting to your ability and trying to improve that ability. Someone watching that practice session (secretly so they don't influence you) would get a very good read on your skills. They would see plenty of repetition of you executing your shooting skills. Maybe you sometimes push in training and make mistakes. Perhaps you shoot more conservatively to try to lock down good scores. Sure, those things could happen, but it would be apparent to an observer when you are pushing or laying back a little.

However, in a match, people tend to approach it differently because it is "for real." Maybe your friend talks you into a goofy stage plan. Maybe you see a shooter that you perceive as fast smash a stage, and it influences you to start pushing beyond your capabilities. Maybe you are shooting a stage and start mashing the trigger throwing multiple rounds at a piece of steel. The fact that you know there is an audience watching you miss that piece of steel repeatedly definitely doesn't help you hit it with your follow up shots.

Just knowing someone is keeping score is going to change your behavior. You start second-guessing yourself on stage plans. You start worrying about being "fast enough." You see a moving target sequence and then start thinking about how the "other guys" will shoot the sequence, instead of just picking an order you are comfortable with. As you can see, competition is going to change your approach, whether you want it to or not.

The best-case scenario when you are shooting a stage is to shoot it like you would if it wasn't a competition. You shoot the stage free of distraction, expectation, or judgment. This is why the advice to "just shoot" is so common. If you can "just shoot" then you are going to be ok.

The key element to "just shooting" is the powerful mental training that takes place long before the match, during the match, and after the match. There are a lot of ideas or concepts that top performers have internalized during their training. Adopting these ideas and genuinely believing them is extremely helpful. I will make a list of a few common beliefs that many of the top shooters hang on to. I wouldn't say that any one of these ideas is universal, but there are some common themes you should pay attention to. I would pick one or two off this list and start internalizing them.

### "Call Your Shots"

One of the more common axioms in shooting is to "call your shots." This means see where each shot is going as you are shooting it by using the sights or dot. This does not mean looking for holes in the target after the shot—that is way too slow, and you should know where the shot went based upon where the sights were lined up when the shot broke. This is excellent advice, especially for someone that is predisposed to shoot faster in a match than their ability allows. If you call each shot as you shoot it, then you are never going to be outshooting your sights.

**"Nobody Else Cares about Your Shooting"**
Some of the best advice new shooters can get is that nobody really cares about their shooting at a match. That might sound a little bit rude, but it isn't meant to be taken that way. The match director at my first match told the group of new shooters, "Nobody will remember your score at your first match, they will only remember you if you do something unsafe."

New shooters should understand that people aren't paying attention to them individually or making any judgments about them as a person when they are shooting. Nobody really cares about your score. The expectation is that newer shooters aren't really going to be relevant from a competitive perspective. This is valuable for new shooters to understand so they can focus on learning the game and navigating the match safely. They absolutely shouldn't worry about other people's opinions or expectations.

**"You Are Fast Enough"**
There are many shooters out there who can shoot extremely quickly during training but feel rushed in a match. They make mistakes induced by rushing or hurrying their way through a stage. The message that these shooters need to take to heart is that they are already fast enough. They don't need to do anything special when they are at a match. Their stage times will be just fine.

**"If You Shoot Slowly It Doesn't Matter How Accurate You Are"**
Many shooters have a natural tendency to aim carefully and avoid mistakes when shooting a match. The desire to

avoid mistakes is so strong that they simply take no risk. The scoring system for practical shooting is set up so that the winning strategy is to shoot right on the edge of your ability. If you fall off the edge, you will have misses or no-shoot hits. If you crash and burn on a stage, you will have a hard time winning the match. However, if you shoot slow and safe, your accuracy becomes irrelevant because you can't win anyway since you're too slow. This is helpful advice for those that are predisposed never to make mistakes, but always feel too slow.

### "Don't Shoot Like a Coward"

Similar to the prior statement about slow shooting making your accuracy irrelevant, "don't shoot like a coward" is speaking to the idea that you can't win anything of note without taking some risk. Again, shooters are rewarded for performing at the limit of their capabilities in a match, not for being the most cautious. We discussed risk management earlier, and that should be taken as the need to mitigate likely risks that can impact your score negatively, not trying to eliminate all risk from your plan. You need to take SOME risks, just smart risks, and not dumb ones.

### "It Doesn't Matter What Anyone Else Does"

One thing I told myself hundreds of times on the road to winning my first Nationals was that it doesn't really matter what anyone else does in the match. I adopted a strategy that I knew would produce optimal scores for myself, but I also know the realities of feeling pressured to race with other people on every single stage. The fact is, you know what is going to produce good results for you and you know what you are comfortable with. If you have taken the time to understand the game and understand yourself, then it really doesn't matter what anyone else is doing, it matters what you do.

### State of Observation

The ideal state of shooting a stage is an empty conscious mind that is simply observing what is happening around it. Think about doing some task that you are well-trained to do. If you are at work, you are maybe knocking out some task you have done thousands of times while you are devoting 100 percent of your conscious attention to listening to a podcast. This is the ideal state of mind for your shooting.

You simply stop directing every part of your shooting with your conscious brain and sit back and observe the shooting as it happens. I wouldn't exactly recommend listening to a podcast while you are on a stage, but you get the idea. You are allowing yourself to shoot, and that's it.

# PART 8
# TRACKING SCORES

# CHAPTER 27
# TRACKING SCORES

For advanced shooters in specific situations, it can sometimes be helpful to know how to track scores. For most competitors in practical shooting, this isn't really a necessity or helpful. That having been said, it should be an interesting window into the thinking of higher-level shooters and give some insight into how to approach larger matches.

"Tracking Scores" is the process by which you follow the scores of yourself and your rival shooters during the match and make adjustments to your stage strategy and shooting pace while you shoot. This requires quite a lot of you as a shooter, so it limits the scenarios where this is applicable. It can't be said enough that this section is just informational for most of the readers. This isn't something that is easy for a B- or C-class shooter to apply in their own matches, but later on it may become useful.

First, you need to know both your scores and your rival's scores as you are shooting. This has gotten easier in recent years with the popularity of digital scoring, but even so, you probably won't be able to see updated scores on a stage-by-stage basis. This requires the ability to estimate the scores in your head as you move through the match, and then verify with actual scoring updates as those become available.

Once you have estimated the scores, you need to have the ability to change strategy as you go through the stages. Again, this is easier said than done. Most people are simply not able to "push" without causing a train wreck or shoot "conservatively" without slowing their shooting pace to a crawl. It may sound like an easy thing to do, but rest assured that without substantial amounts of training and checking your results when using different approaches to the stages, it just isn't advisable to start making these strategy changes.

With those caveats out of the way, we can move on to how this really works. Essentially what tracking scores allows you to do is to manage your risk level as you go through the match. I used this method to win a USPSA Nationals. The basic theory is simply when you are behind, you take calculated risks to catch up. When you are tied, you either wait for your opponent to make a mistake and fall back, or you push to get ahead. When you are ahead, you minimize the risk level, so you stay ahead. It is that simple.

When you are tracking scores this way, your thinking should be in terms of match points, and not one shooter's match percentage as opposed to the other. Match points are much easier to deal with, so they are preferred. The method I use for scoring in my head is to use a system where I track match points relative to someone else.

So, for example, I might say, "I am 20 points behind Joe." That is all the information I need to have. I don't care what the percentage of points is or anything like that.

The aggregate points shot or match time doesn't make any difference. The only thing that matters is the match point difference between one person and the other at any point during the match.

After the conclusion of a stage, I can then estimate the relative change in the points situation from the results of that stage. There are two main methods I use to estimate. These methods are simplified so I can do them quickly in my head, and they are not entirely accurate. Due to the way in which match points are actually calculated, you need more information than is likely available—primarily the "High Hit Factor" on a stage—in order to know the exact points that each shooter will get in the final results. When shooters are spread out all across the match, you may not know who really won a particular stage.

One method to do the estimation is to note the difference in points and time, and the other is to use the hit factor on the stage. Let's look at an example:

- Shooter A (shooting Production minor) has a 6.3 hit factor, a time of 22.5 seconds, and dropped 18 points on the stage.
- Shooter B (also Production minor) has a 6.5 hit factor, a time of 24.1 seconds, and dropped 4 points.

(Note: I rounded the hit factor to one decimal place.)
To roughly estimate the change in points here, I can use the points/time method or the hit factor method.

Going by points and time, I see that on a roughly six-factor stage, shooter A was about 1.5 seconds faster. This means they picked up approximately 9 points (6 points per second times 1.5 seconds). They dropped 14 points more as far as accuracy is concerned . . . so they ended up five points behind in total (14 minus 9). So, our rough guesstimate here is that Shooter A dropped back about five match points.

Going by hit factor instead, we take a 6.3 hit factor (the lower factor) and divide by 6.5. In this case, the shooter with the 6.3 factor shot about 97 percent of the score of the other shooter. The stage has 160 points available. 97 percent of 160 is about 155 . . . meaning that the lower factor shooter lost about five match points compared to the other.

This math is rough, and again, other shooters taking stage wins tend to "compress" the results making the differences between the two shooters' scores very muted.

Once you understand the basic math going on here, then you are ready to start tracking scores. I recommend you start practicing this skill by squadding with your rivals at a club match. Just keep track of the scores in your head and compare the results at the end of the match. With time and practice, you can learn to "know" the scores before they are calculated, and this can prove to be an important tool in certain situations.

If you are sitting on a 30-point lead against your main rival going into the last stage of your club match (for example), then pretty much all you have to do is shoot the final stage without falling on your face, and you are going to win. There really isn't anything that someone of similar skill level is going to be able to do to pick up 30 points on you if you shoot the stage decently. This knowledge is valuable in that you know you don't need to do anything crazy or silly to win. You can avoid doing something you are uncomfortable with to lock down a match win. This is just one example, and it illustrates the concept of how you can use your knowledge of the match score during the match to make better decisions on strategy.

# CHAPTER 28

# SQUADDING

Practical Shooting is an individual sport. You are the only one who affects your score, yet you have to work as a team to reset the stages. You need to be respectful of the others on the squad, or they won't want to squad with you in the future. Most people understand the logistics of squadding, but relatively few understand the etiquette. This is especially true for newer shooters. There isn't a formal system where these things get explained to people. This section will discuss the expectations for how you should behave on the range.

We have all been in a squad where everyone seems to pull their weight. Things seem to run smoothly, and it makes the day more enjoyable. We shake hands at the end of the day and make mental notes to squad with those people again in the future since we had such a great time.

Conversely, a bad experience with a squad can make for a long day. There may be a competitor who is unnecessarily argumentative, doesn't help, or otherwise causes problems. If there is miserable weather on top of this, it can feel like a nightmare. You might tell yourself, "I will never squad with that person again."

If anything, this section should help you manage your expectations with others and hopefully not be "that guy" to other people.

## Squad Jobs

There are a few jobs that need to get done in a squad. In a typical club match, you might see a person assume every role at some point in the match. You might see other people just do one job for the duration of the match. Most squad members commonly expect to shift between resetting and shooting with maybe another job sprinkled in. The jobs are as follows:

**Range Officer**—The Range Officer is the person holding the timer. This person runs shooters through the stage and makes scoring calls. This position is pivotal in that it tends to determine the flow of the squad through the match. A competent Range Officer will run things smoothly and quickly. A bad Range Officer can slow things down dramatically. This position is typically reserved for more experienced shooters, likely those certified as Range Officers in the sport, although in smaller club matches this may not always be the case.

**Scorekeeper**—The scorekeeper holds the scoring device and serves as a secondary Range Officer. They can and will make calls on their own, or assist the primary Range Officer in making calls. The scorekeeper also manages the shooting order and reads the order off with regularity, so everyone knows what is happening with the order of shooters and when they are coming up in the order.

**Resetters**—Resetting things by pasting targets, picking up steel, resetting moving targets, and repainting steel is the job that most shooters on the squad will find themselves doing. There tends to be more than just one person doing this job. Usually, at least three people are doing this in order to help things move quickly.

**Magazine Pickup**—Someone usually assists the shooter by picking up magazines for them on their behalf. In the event that for some reason, the brass needs to get picked up all the time, someone will almost always help the shooter with that as well.

**Shooter**—It is helpful to think of shooting as one of the jobs you need to do on a squad. You should be ready to go when you are called, and your visualization and preparation should be completed ahead of time. The fact that you have a job to do as a shooter should always be in the back of your mind. No one likes the shooter who is chronically unprepared and causes constant delays for the squad every time it's his turn to shoot. Think about the guy who walks up to the line and then realizes he forgot to refill his magazines after the last stage. Or the guy who walks to the line with his jacket on and then realizes he needs to take it off before he shoots. Or the guy who tries to do another full walkthrough of the stage after the RO has told him to "Make Ready," because he's still deciding how he wants to shoot the stage. Don't be that guy.

## Match Flow

The match flows in predictable ways. We are going to describe here the "standard" flow for USPSA club matches. Things work differently at other matches and may work differently in different regions. The USPSA club match is, in our estimation, the most complicated situation as far as squadding is concerned. If you are ok at a USPSA club event, you are probably ok anywhere.

The most important thing for anyone shooting a USPSA match is that they do their share of the work when it is their time to do their share of the work. If they don't do what they are supposed to do to support the squad, then things drag on forever, and tempers start to flare up.

As your squad works its way through an event, people have different roles and responsibilities, primarily determined by the order that people shoot in. Generally speaking, people get divided up into two sets. There is one set of people who are either about to shoot (on deck, in-the-hole), currently shooting, or just shot. The squad should expect virtually nothing from those people. They should be focused on their preparation and shooting.

The other group, the people who are not shooting, up to shoot, or just shot, are the people who are supposed to be doing the work to keep things moving.

The key piece of information, the most important thing that you as a shooter should always be keeping track of, is the "shooting order." Standard practice is that shooting order is established by mutual consent before the match starts. Typically, the shooting order is alphabetical by first or last name. The person who shoots first on a stage typically moves to the bottom of the order for the next stage. It's common for the order to drop either one or two shooters down the list to determine who shoots first on the next stage. The squad will shoot in the same order throughout the match, and you should make an effort to know your place in the order as well as a few other people's places ahead of you in the order as well. The idea is that when you are called up to shoot, it should never be a surprise. You need to be switched on and paying attention to when people are shooting so you can both do your part to help the squad and be ready to shoot when you are supposed to. Getting caught by surprise by the shooting order can lead to a bad performance on your part, or lead to holding things up as you scramble to get ready. Neither of those things are good.

The shooting order is usually read off by the score-keeper or the Range Officer for the squad, or another des-ignated squad member. At many clubs, the "in charge" person is just an experienced person that informally is running the squad. At some clubs, it may be a more formal responsibility. It doesn't really make much of a difference, you should just be paying attention to the order. You prob-ably want to physically see the shooting order for yourself and give it a couple quick reads so you know where you are in the order, and where a couple of your buddies are so you can coordinate video or whatever you might want to do.

When the shooting order is read, you will hear terms like:

"The shooter" is the person currently up to shoot.

"On-deck" means the next shooter.

"In-the-hole" means shooter after next.

"In-the-deep-hole" means two shooters after next – not common, but some clubs use this term.

Once you're "in-the-hole" or within a few shooters of it being your turn, it's ok to give up whatever other job you were doing. You shouldn't have to worry about serv-ing as an RO, scorekeeper, or resetting. Take the time you need to double-check that your mags are filled, dry fire in the safe area, apply a grip enhancer, visualize your stage plan, and do anything you need to do to get ready for your run.

Be mindful of the shooting order and aware of what others are doing before you walk up to them and start talking. Pay attention to the behavior and body language of the other competitors. If you see someone standing off to the side with their eyes closed, you probably should leave them alone. Generally speaking, you should not be too chatty with someone when they are "on deck" because their focus is going to be elsewhere, and they don't want or need your distraction.

When you are up to shoot, and the person just before you has finished their stage run and unloaded, then the stage is "yours." You essentially "own" the stage at that point. People get very annoyed, and rightly so, if you are walking on a stage they "own." Do not be that guy. With the exception of people resetting or scoring the stage, only the "on-deck shooter" has any business anywhere in the shooting area after the shooter has finished their run and the stage is being scored. This is something that you might see from an inexperienced shooter who doesn't "get it" yet, and it's common and appropriate for the RO or another experienced shooter to correct this behavior by letting them know it's not ok to be walking through a stage that you are not the next shooter on. Unfortunately, you might also see this from an experienced shooter who thinks their need to walk through is more important than the current shooter. This guy is a jerk. His buddy, the mega-jerk, is the one who walks over to the NEXT stage that he's not currently on yet and starts walking through it in the middle of another squad. Yes, this happens, and these are the guys mentioned earlier who no one wants to squad with, for obvious reasons.

If you just completed shooting a stage, after "unload and show clear," it's a good idea to walk with the Range Officer as they score the targets. Do not worry about your magazines; someone on your squad will likely pick them up for you, or you can gather them up yourself at the end if necessary. It is absolutely ok to ask the RO if you see a questionable call or have a question about why they made the call they did. Range Officers are human, and humans make mistakes. They might not see a bullet hole you see, or they might accidentally call a score incorrectly. Getting clarification for something you don't understand is going to help you in the future. Note that this is NOT the same as the guy who challenges every call, thinks every Mike is really a double, etc. That guy is going to annoy the RO. If you are polite and have legitimate questions for the RO, virtually no one will have a problem with that. After all, it's YOUR score that is being determined, not anyone else's, so you have the most vested interest in making sure it's correct.

Reloading your magazines and getting all of your gear ready for the next stage should be your first priority after you are finished shooting and your score has been entered. Develop a system and an order you do these things in, a standard routine. By creating a habit, you will be less likely to forget anything. Some people have a habit of never putting a mag on their belt after a stage until it has been refilled. Some take every magazine off their belt and check each one before they put them back on their belt.

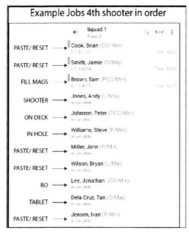

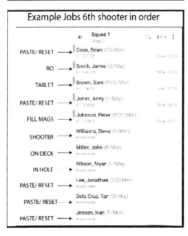

*Figure 12: Example of how the "jobs" change based on the flow of the shooting order. Everyone doing their part helps the match run smoothly.*

Make sure each magazine is filled to the correct capacity and take the magazine apart to brush it or wipe it off if necessary. If you are shooting on a range that has a lot of sand or is very dusty, you might disassemble any magazine that hits the ground for cleaning before the next stage. The actual specifics aren't as critical as making sure you have a system and a routine that gets all of your gear ready, and you have the feeling of always being prepared when it's your turn to shoot.

Typically, you should expect to shoot in squads of 10–12 competitors. I have seen squads as small as three and a group as large as 30 at a club level event. However, 10–12 is the norm. With a 10-person group, there is going to be a Range Officer, a Scorekeeper, and about four people resetting the stage and picking things up. This leaves four people that are in-the-hole, on-deck, shooting, or just shot. As the squad moves through the shooting order, people smoothly hand off jobs from one person to the next. The Range Officer who is about to be on deck will hand the timer to someone else. The score-keeper will manage the scoring tablet the same way. A good squad has lots of communication, and people make sure that someone else takes their job from them at the appropriate time. There is a lot of common sense at work, and as long as all of the squad mates are on the same page as far as duties and roles, it can run like a well-oiled machine.

When everyone on your squad has shot that stage, your squad moves to the next stage and begins the stage briefing and walkthrough there. You get a fixed amount of time for walkthroughs at this point, but it won't be most people's first look at the stage, they either walked it earlier that day or the day before. Many people will be at the point of making small decisions such as deciding on their activator sequence or something like that. Usually, the Range Officer will read the written stage briefing aloud and clarify the procedure for the stage. Note that it is expected that all members of the squad listen to this briefing, as it may contain important safety-related information or other information related to the smooth operation of the stage. This might include information on how to reset activating targets, listing prohibited actions on the stage, and specifying the order in which targets will be scored so that no one resets ahead of the score being recorded. Therefore, anyone who is walking through the stage when the stage briefing is announced is expected to stop what they are doing and attend the briefing. If you have to be yelled at twice by the RO to stop walking the stage and come back to the stage briefing, you're being "that guy."

During the squad walkthrough, it's definitely ok to ask for help if you have questions. It can be intimidating for newer shooters to ask for help because they don't want to feel like they're interrupting or being a nuisance. It's fair to say that the majority of the people you meet at matches will be willing to help you and answer your questions. Be mindful of not stopping them in the middle of walking through the stage themselves. Ask your questions respectfully, and you'll have no problem finding someone willing to help you. People tend to be pretty chatty during the squad walkthrough time, so take advantage of it if you want to.

You should have a general idea at this point, but there are a few points of etiquette that probably need to be addressed. Not all of these things are true in all locations, there are regional differences, but this section should give you a baseline for how to behave in certain situations.

# CHAPTER 29

# INTEGRITY

One issue that can make you a lot of enemies in a hurry is to act in bad faith in a match. Arguing for scoring calls you don't deserve, trying to get a reshoot on a stage you messed up, or trying to get a stage you did poorly on pulled from the match are examples of acting in bad faith. There are extreme examples such as shooters deliberately altering scores or otherwise cheating, but those are so extreme and obviously wrong we shouldn't need to address them here.

Nobody likes being around someone who argues every call or acts like a jerk to their fellow competitors. It is highly unlikely that there will be a face-to-face confrontation if you act in bad faith, but rest assured people will talk about it behind your back and not want to squad with you. It isn't always the most mature or adult system, but the informal system of ostracizing people who don't act right is pretty much par for the course at USPSA club events.

A good example of acting in bad faith is the infamous "double" call. Someone has a single target with one hole in it, and they argue that actually, two bullets went through that hole in order to avoid being scored a miss. Now, "doubles" do occasionally happen. Someone might actually believe that they had a double, they called the shots and are certain that both bullets were headed for the target. There is really nothing wrong with arguing for what you believe in. If you clearly state your case and try to get the Range Officer to see things your way, then you aren't doing anything wrong. Range Officers have a procedure for measuring "double" calls using bullet overlays, but generally they won't do it unless you ask for a call on it. If you think it's legitimate, ask for the call.

There are some people who, as a matter of procedure, will ALWAYS argue for a double in the case that they are being called for a miss on the target. Without fail, they will argue incessantly as long as people let them. This type of behavior is generally considered to be extremely annoying. This person will hold up the match to argue for a scoring call they know, or should know, that they do not deserve. It can't be said enough, do not be this person. Don't be afraid to argue for what you believe you deserve, but do not argue everything just in hopes of getting something you don't deserve. You will lose friends very quickly.

# CHAPTER 30
# RANGE OFFICER ISSUES

Personality clashes are going to happen at matches occasionally, and they are logically more frequent when dealing with someone acting as a Range Officer, due to the position of authority the RO is in. If you have a personality clash with another shooter on the squad, you can just ignore each other for the most part, but everyone has to interact with the Range Officer. Range Officers tend to be the more experienced people, and sometimes this experience carries negative tendencies in addition to the positive value of experience. RO's are competitors and humans, just like you, which means that they can have any type of personality. Some want to be everyone's best friend, and others seem, inexplicably, to be annoyed that they are even at the match.

Clashes with an RO can be due to many factors, but most likely due to a call you don't agree with, or with the RO's way of running the squad. A good example of this is an RO who rushes through the range commands and short-beeps every shooter because he's focused almost exclusively on how fast the squad is run. You may feel that the RO is rushing you in your stage preparation. You may not understand something or not know something that the RO feels you are supposed to know, and the RO may be impatient with you due to this. Or the RO may just have poor attention to detail and make bad calls by not giving the targets a thorough examination.

The best way to handle an issue with a Range Officer is directly. Addressing whatever the issue is up front to make sure you understand what calls are being made and why, is the best practice. If you feel the RO is rushing you in your stage preparation, it's totally ok to address this and ask the RO to give you the time you need for your prep. After the "Make Ready" command, the time is yours and you can use it as you see fit to prepare yourself. Often, the RO doesn't even realize he's rushing people since he's just focused on keeping the match moving along.

If you encounter a Range Officer who seems quick to DQ people or appears to be happy to call penalties, this is an RO who is not really good for the sport and you are probably best served to avoid squadding with that person in the future.

Please note, this is different from an RO who is firm but fair. Ideally, you should get a sense from the RO that they don't really care what the scoring outcome is, they are just calling things as they see them per the rules, right down the middle. An RO who is firm with everyone, but also fair, is the type of person that you want to seek out and squad with in the future. Particularly at Major Matches, this is the type of RO that you want. A good RO will make the match run smoothly and ensure that everyone is treated fairly in the match.

# CHAPTER 31

# DISQUALIFICATIONS

It is highly likely during your shooting career that you will, at some point, experience a DQ. You will likely witness another shooter DQ at some point during a match. Neither of these events is really anything to be alarmed about, but they can be sensitive situations.

First, if you get DQ'd during a match, you should stay calm as the process plays out. Usually, there is a conversation with a Range Officer about what happened, and then possibly a higher-level Range Official will want to talk to you about it afterward. Stay cool, understand the reason for the DQ, ask for clarification if necessary, and argue firmly and politely if you disagree with the call for a legitimate reason. You will likely not win the argument, and there isn't anything else you can really do about it. If it's a major match and you're positive you are in the right, then arbitration may be an option. If it's a club match, just let it go.

Everyone has been or likely will be DQ'd at some point if they shoot long enough, and it doesn't need to be a big deal. The main trap you want to avoid is blowing the DQ up into a bigger deal than it is. I would advise not taking the issue to social media to talk about it under most circumstances. That just tends to highlight an issue when there is really nothing to be gained from talking about it with a broader audience.

You should understand what got you DQ'd and address the training deficiency that led to the problem. You want to not only BE safe but try to give the appearance of safety as much as you can as you shoot. Training with that in mind to avoid future DQs is a good thing. An example of this would be if you have a tendency to have your trigger finger hanging just outside the trigger guard next to the trigger on your reloads, it will LOOK like your finger is on the trigger when viewed from the opposite side. An RO may see this and DQ you for having your finger on the trigger. It wasn't, and you can argue it, but you probably won't win because it's a judgement call on the part of the RO. A better solution would be to work on that in training and get your trigger finger indexed up against the frame so it's clearly outside the trigger guard no matter who is watching.

If you see someone else get DQ'd for one reason or another, it's usually best for you to stay out of the issue. You should jump in to report what you witnessed if it is relevant to the issue, but generally speaking DQ's get issued at the RO's discretion, and nothing you saw is really going to matter anyway. People might get angry or worked up as DQ's get sorted out, so not getting involved is usually best.

If you happen to get a video of yourself DQ-ing, it is not advised to post it online. The video of your DQ going on the internet just highlights the issue with no real upside. I've never seen a positive outcome from that, and it tends to ignite people's anger even more if there was a contentious situation. It is best to have the discussion in person at the time of the DQ and then drop it.

If you happen to get a video of someone else's DQ, I would offer it up to the shooter. If that person doesn't want the footage for whatever reason, then I personally would delete it from my device. Spreading that footage around would likely be viewed as an attempt to humiliate or embarrass someone about an unfortunate situation that pretty much everyone has been through.

# CHAPTER 32
# OTHER UNSPOKEN "RULES"

**Giving Advice**

You should use caution when choosing to give advice to people. Shooting tends to draw a diverse set of personalities, and a common thread with many of these personalities is that they are "type A" people who don't really care what anyone else thinks. Unsolicited advice is not something I would recommend giving to anyone. The exception to this rule is when you see someone who is obviously struggling, and they look like they could use some help. Giving that person a bit of advice would likely be appreciated, especially if this is a newer shooter who needs the guidance. It's best to ask, "Hey it looks like you might need some help, can I offer you some advice on this?" You're a hero to most new shooters at that point—be that guy.

**Borrowing Gear/Ammo**

The general rule I would give to most people is that if they need some sort of loaner gear or need some ammunition, they are going to be able to get help at a match. I have found the shooting community to be very generous when it comes to people needing to borrow something or people who need a spare part for one reason or another.

If you need anything or have something break in a match, speak up. If anyone has the extra fiber you need for your sight or has the twenty additional rounds you need to shoot the last stage, or really anything within reason, it is a safe bet that somebody will help you out at a match. Obviously, you don't want to abuse this situation, but do not hesitate to ask around for something you need. I would also recommend returning the favor or paying it forward to other people when you have a chance.

## Taking Video

At this point, it is expected that you will likely want a video of yourself shooting or, at some point, take a video of someone else. This is a normal thing, but there are a few informal guidelines you want to pay attention to.

First, pay attention to safety considerations when videoing someone. If you are going to video someone shooting a stage and you plan to walk downrange into where the shooting area is, then you want to make sure that other people around you, especially the RO's, aren't surprised by you doing that. The best practice is to ask the Range Officer what they want you to do. They might say, "yeah, that's fine, just stay behind me." That lets the RO know that you are respecting them and not going to get further downrange than they want you to get.

If someone asks you to video them and you can do it, you should say yes. Make sure you figure out how their device works before that person walks away from you. Then pay attention to the shooting order to make sure you don't miss the chance to video the person you are helping out. Generally speaking, people are happy with a video that shows them from the time their gun is loaded and goes into the holster (indicating they are ready) until a couple seconds after their last shot is fired. They don't need to see any more than that, and they don't need to see the thirty seconds they spent "making ready." You should strive to video someone from their feet to their head so they can see they full picture of what they are doing (unless asked otherwise).

When asking someone to video you, try to pick someone who is in a convenient place given the shooting order. Asking the person that directly follows you in the order would be quite inconsiderate. Asking someone opposite you in the order is usually the best way to go. Just make sure you explain what you want on the video and make sure they know how to use your device, and you should be fine.

### Resetting the Stage

When you are working the job of resetting the stage, there are a few things you want to watch out for to ensure everything goes smoothly.

First and foremost, do not get ahead of the scoring Range Officer. Absolutely make certain that a target is scored, and the score is agreed to, before you paste or reset the target. This means that if you aren't sure if a target is scored or not, ask someone. If the target has been scored in a way that you think the shooter is likely to object to, make sure that the shooter is aware of the score and has a chance to lodge any objection they have to the score, before you reset the target. Commonly, misses and no-shoot hits are left for the shooter to look at to confirm they don't have an issue with the score that is being called. Also, if you see an obvious scoring error that was made, don't reset the target and get the RO's attention on it. DO NOT touch the target at all in that case. For example, if the RO called Alpha-Delta, but there is also a hit in the bottom corner of the C-zone that the RO didn't see, alert the RO so the shooter gets the correct score.

Another vital thing to pay attention to when resetting is how any activating or moving target with a potentially complicated procedure for reset is handled. If you don't know how something gets set up, then ask someone and make sure you know how to do it properly. Incorrectly set moving targets are a common cause of reshoots, and you don't want to be the person causing that to happen.

Another good practice when doing the reset is to make sure you look around as you exit the stage. You will probably find targets that didn't get pasted on occasion, and you want to address that situation, so it doesn't cause a problem for the next shooter.

## Talking Smack

People at some clubs talk a lot of smack to each other. Being on a squad with the authors, you would almost think we are enemies. That, of course, isn't the case . . . we just like to talk smack. It's a sign of camaraderie and helps keep friends relaxed and having fun.

The best way to get integrated into your club and get along with other people is to avoid talking smack to people you don't know. It's also best to avoid talking smack to your friends around people you don't know. It helps prevent them from getting the wrong impression about what you are doing. This isn't a rule I have always observed myself, and it has gotten me into trouble from time to time.

## Talking to a Competitor After They're Done Shooting

In the moments immediately after someone's stage run, they don't have a lot of time for small talk. You should avoid speaking to a competitor about their run until after the scoring process is complete and the score is agreed to. This is just common courtesy for that person to let them handle the task at hand before you start chatting with them.

If someone has a bad run (not a run that YOU think is bad, but a run that THEY are unhappy with), then you should give them some space for a while. It's almost like someone died when a shooter who trains all the time to do well crashes and burns on a stage. That person is going to be upset. That person should be upset. If they didn't care, then why are they trying so hard?

Just give them a little space for a while, and once they start smiling again it is a safe time to re-engage with them.

## Local Flavor

Certain things are ok in some areas and some clubs, and not ok in others.

For example: At my club, if I see a no-shoot hit on a target while I am resetting the stage and I point that out to the Range Officer, that would be totally normal. It would be expected, in fact. Everyone is expected to assist the RO to get the shooter the correct score. And the shooter might be upset with the no-shoot hit, but they won't be upset with me for pointing it out.

At other clubs, pointing out a no-shoot to the Range Officer in exactly the same set of circumstances would be seen as an unsportsmanlike move. The prevailing view at this club may be that the score the shooter gets is between the RO and the shooter, and it's none of your business.

You will find that local custom and flavor absolutely has an influence on what is ok and what is not ok at a particular club, in various aspects of how matches are operated. Following the lead of more experienced people and asking lots of questions is the best practice to navigate these sorts of situations.

# PART 9
# AFTER THE MATCH

# CHAPTER 33

# ANALYSIS AND IMPROVEMENT

So, you finished the match and have a rank and percentage you finished in. What do you do with that information? How can it help you? Before you knew the score, you probably already had a feeling about how things went. Those feelings can sometimes tell you things the numbers don't show.

The first thing to accept is that no one has a "perfect" match at any level. As your skill increases, the severity and frequency of the mistakes should decrease. Mistakes will bother you regardless of the level of your skill, and the frustration with mistakes will probably increase as you get better. If you see a new shooter who makes lot of mistakes, and blows a gasket about every mistake they make, that shooter is in for a long and painful ride in the sport, if they even stay in the sport long-term.

You can learn a lot from looking at the match results, and you can find data to make yourself believe anything you want to. The whole point of this section is helping you analyze your performance realistically so you can develop a plan for improvement.

The first thing I look at is how I compare in overall stage times for all of the stages combined for my division, and in particular for the other shooters at my same skill level. The aggregate time available in the scoring software is very useful in this way. In a general sense, am I fast, slow, or am I finishing close on time to where everyone else is? You might have had a gun malfunction or an issue on a stage that cost you a few seconds, so take that into consideration. Your competitors might have had the same sorts of issues. Don't read too much into any one data point, just keep an eye on things match after match and try to pay attention to the trends. If you're consistently one of the fastest shooters, then you don't likely need to work on getting even faster, it's more likely you need to work on dropping fewer points. The opposite is also true, if you're a turtle who is always high on points but slow on time, you'll need to work on getting faster.

The next thing I look at is how I compared in points. I compare my alpha count to the winner (if it wasn't me) and the rest of the field of "relevant" competitors to my skill level to see how I compare. How many C's, D's, and misses did I have compared to everyone else? I don't get too concerned about the count at this point, I am just looking for a general feeling. For the most part, you should be able to complete a normal five or six stage club match with very few, if any, penalties. If you have never in your life shot a match without having a miss, that is something that you should pay attention to. If you rarely shoot a miss at your matches, you should pay attention to that data point as well. Use your analysis of your points compared to other shooters to inform you about what you need to work on in training.

Looking at each stage result separately gives you a lot of data, but you should be very careful not to read too much into this data. I have found that shooters tend to have the ability to interpret stage results in any way that makes them happy. For example, they may be happy they beat X shooter on some stage or did Y thing on some other stage. In reality, those data points may mean nothing. Your rival maybe had some issue on a stage that you are celebrating beating them on. You should take a very measured approach to reading stage results and look for overall trends rather than cherry-picking data that lines up with what you want to believe. With that caution in mind, there are some things you can look for on stage results that can help inform your training goals moving forward.

If you tend to do well or do poorly on a particular type of stage, you should key in on that. Stand and shoot classifiers are one stage type that people commonly either struggle with or excel at. It just depends on the person. There are stages with lots of running, stages with long/ tight shots, stages with lots of movers, whatever. You can categorize the stages any way you like and read the data that way to look for a pattern. The nice thing is that if you decide what type of stage some random stage is, then that is the type it is to you. Nobody else can define that for you, and the kind of stage you feel you are dealing with is the type of stage it is. Remember, you tend to be battling your own feelings as much as the stages in competition.

You also need to remember the strategy you used on a stage you are analyzing. Here's an example: Imagine a stage with very difficult partials on almost every target. Your strategy on that stage might have been to just get through it without getting a penalty, and you held in the "center of brown" to accomplish that goal. In doing so, you might have more C's than some of the other competitors, but you got through without a penalty. In that example, the alpha count isn't as important because your goal was to shoot the stage clean without a penalty. Maybe on a high hit factor stage, you only had one C, but you were five seconds slower than everyone else. That helps locate a speed deficiency on easy targets.

The difficulty of the match has a tremendous impact on the results. A very low difficulty match with lots of easy close targets will cause the results to be very tightly compressed because it's easier, and most people can perform relatively well. You will probably have a higher percentage in an easier match.

You will see more separation in the results in matches that have a balanced test of skills. If the match has close fast shooting, far targets with tight partials, one-handed shooting, activated targets, lots of opportunities for shooting on the move, etc., the match will expose any deficiency in the competitor's abilities. Those deficiencies will have an effect on the results and create separation between the competitors.

The important thing for your analysis is that you understand what you are dealing with when you look at match results. An "easy" match that you shoot at your home range should produce the strongest possible performance. A Nationals or World Championship shot someplace you have never been is likely going to expose more of your deficiencies. Another way to think about this is if you have lots of penalties and make lots of mistakes at your "easy" club matches, you have zero chance of shooting better than that at a major match. You should be working toward maximizing your performance at the easiest matches as the first step in your development. Proving you can do it there will build the confidence needed to start working toward replicating that performance level at more important matches.

After you have looked at the match result data, think of the big picture of your shooting. You might have had a really excellent stage and an awful stage. I would just dismiss those highs and lows and look at your shooting as a whole. You have to realize you can't shoot the entire match at 100 percent, and you will make mistakes. How does the bulk of your shooting look? Don't focus on one bobbled unloaded start, but which skills are you falling short on, time and time again? Those repeated deficiencies are the things you should key in on. Keep notes on these analyses over time to look for trends and work on any deficiencies you find in your upcoming training sessions.

When I look at someone's match video, I won't pick out the one time it looked like they struggled on a draw, when 98 percent of the time it looks good. Instead, I look for things that happen over and over that will yield the highest reward from focusing on them in training. Imagine a person is late getting the gun up when they get to a position at least once or twice a stage, but they drop a magazine while reloading the gun one time in the entire match. Their gun handling looks solid, other than dropping that magazine one time. That person would see a much higher return on time investment from working on having the gun up and ready to shoot when they enter a position instead of working on mag changes for a month to address an issue that only happened once this year. Unfortunately, small mistakes are going to happen, and sometimes these are not indicative of your skill as a whole. Look at your shooting as one big picture and constantly work to improve the whole machine, focusing particularly on deficiencies you note in your match performances.

# CHAPTER 34

# ORGANIZING YOUR LIFE AND SHOOTING

If you want to set your goals without disrupting your life or burning out, it is absolutely essential that you do a bit of planning and get things organized. Depending on your goals and participation level, this may mean getting your shooting organized to fit into your life, or it may mean getting your life organized around your shooting goals. It should be obvious that you need to put in the work in order to accomplish anything. What is less obvious is the need to structure your life from the outset, so you make doing the work very low effort and sustainable.

Thinking about these issues ahead of time will help you accomplish your goals, it will help avoid burnout, it will prevent financial or family strains, and it will generally keep you happier. There are many people who fail to plan things out correctly, and halfway through a shooting season they lose the drive to practice. Maybe after they spend $5,000 in the space of a couple months, their spouse gets upset and it starts to cause issues at home. Or maybe they can no longer seem to find the time in their schedule to fit in the training program that they were excited about earlier in the season.

For those of you who are more on the casual side of participating, you should work out what matches are convenient to attend and also sort out range access for occasional training. If you just want to shoot a bit with your friends and have fun, you must not get sucked into over-participating in matches or situations you don't necessarily want to be in. It is easy to have a particular set of goals and then get peer pressured into attending events that don't really serve your goals. Too much of this type of pressure can cause burnout.

For the more serious shooters who are regularly traveling great distances to matches, it is important to pick out events that matter a great deal and then build a plan to attend those events with your shooting in peak form. This means that you don't want to spend six consecutive weeks traveling for major matches just before you show up at USPSA Nationals (for example). Instead, you should have a plan that gets you warmed up for the matches you care about, but still allows you training time between matches to be in peak form. You also need to have a good balance with your family life, and have a financial plan to pay for everything. It can get complicated, and that is why thinking about it early is imperative.

Pick a match schedule that works over the long term. You want to get your life organized so that it actually functions appropriately and still allows you to reach your shooting goals. You don't want to plan for a match season that has you doing club matches every weekend and traveling to ten major competitions while you are simultaneously expecting your first child to be born mid-season. That plan probably isn't going to work out. You would expect there to be quite a lot of relationship stress added in if you do attend that many events.

Someone "biting off more than they can chew" during the early season planning phase means that they will likely burn themselves out mid-season. They may succumb to relationship pressure, or they might get annoyed at the high cost of participation and want to back off their participation dramatically. In any event, these problems are self-induced. You want to avoid them with effective planning.

Try to consider your shooting season as one big picture. There will be times when you are training very heavily, times you are going to matches you consider important, and times that you aren't doing much of anything shooting-related at all. All of these phases are very important. Shooters who skip rest or aren't shooting enough matches leading up to their goal match, or shooters who aren't training regularly all pay for these mistakes in the end.

I tend to structure my shooting season, so I am always productive, but boredom is minimal. There is a preparatory phase at the beginning of the year. I get used to new equipment and make sure I am making enough ammo to get me through the year. I experiment on technique and training changes. This is all happening quite a long time before any important matches for me.

It's very highly beneficial to do your testing of new ideas and equipment long before you are going to be doing it "for real" in a match of consequence. You will probably do a better job of trying new things when you are free of the pressure that will inevitably find you later on in the year when major matches start popping off all over the place. This can take the form of both dry-fire and live-fire training.

It is also wise to have a few matches where you have an opportunity to "warm-up." You shouldn't just save it all up for the few matches you really care about. You should be testing your skills at smaller matches. Club matches are a great way to try new things in a much more friendly and low-pressure environment. Again, make this part of your thinking as you are making a plan for what you are going to do in your shooting season. It's all about priorities, use the minor matches to tune up for the matches that really matter.

Maybe in the mid-season, you are going to do fewer club matches and save more time for training. Most people don't have unlimited time, and a Saturday club match likely means no Saturday practice. After you have tested out some new things and shot matches for a couple months you probably have an idea of some things you want to really drill down on in training to improve. You will probably be better served mid-season by emphasizing training more than matches you don't really care about.

Of course, as the end of your season and your goal match (or matches) approach, then they will likely dominate your time and attention as you prepare to shoot your absolute best during those events. In this phase of your shooting season, I wouldn't be shooting a ton of other matches. Instead, I would be focused on doing plenty of training and making minimal equipment changes, so I am ready to go for the big matches.

Climate is absolutely going to be a consideration as you plan out your season. In climates that have a proper winter, you probably aren't going to be shooting a whole lot outdoors during that time of the year. If you have a brutal summer where you live, you might be adjusting your schedule so you can get to the range before the peak heat of the day or maybe even do less training during that time of the year. In any event, you should be thinking about climate considerations and planning an "off-season" when it makes sense based on the geography of where you live.

I would err on the more conservative side if you are debating about how many matches you want to sign up for. You don't want to feel overwhelmed or unprepared. As you become more experienced, you might want to grow your participation and sign up for more matches the next year.

## Train Easy, Not Hard

The less energy it takes to practice, the more you will be able to do it and want to do it. If it takes you an hour to set up practice and an hour to tear down, you probably won't find yourself wanting to practice every day. Or if you have an hour drive each way to get to the closest outdoor practice range, it ends up being a major event to do live fire training. The amount of effort and time it takes just to get everything ready can play a big part in your schedule. The solution is to make training easy on you.

Instead of dragging out a bunch of props for every practice, maybe you only use three or four target stands and a piece of steel saving you ten minutes in setup time. Then you use a brass chute or tarp to collect your brass, saving you five to ten minutes in cleanup time. Then you acquire a magazine loader and paster gun, which allow you to practice with less effort. All these things save you time and make it more convenient to fit practice into your life.

## Budgeting Time

It's essential to have a realistic and sustainable training routine. You might want to ramp up training a week or two before a major match, but set your normal training schedule to a pace you will enjoy and won't cause you to burn out. Going to train shouldn't be something you always need to force yourself to do. However, you should realize that the top shooters do often go to train when they don't necessarily feel like it.

Set a schedule that fits into your life and still allows you to have time for your family and friends. Just like you budget ammo and time for training, you need to budget time for your other commitments and relationships too. Your schedule should change based upon the season. As spring, summer, and fall get busy with life events, your shooting will also be in full swing. You will likely find yourself with more downtime during the winter or off-season. It's important that you can budget your time so you can train and still have time for family and friends when it matters. Getting pressure on your time from multiple fronts can put you in an uncomfortable situation and take the fun out of training.

One thing that can be helpful when it comes to managing your relationships and time is just having a routine that other people are used to. If you train on Tuesday and Thursday nights and shoot a match every other Sunday, and you keep that schedule for a while, then you are unlikely to catch a lot of flak for it since your family and friends will be used to it.

Something that helps with my routine is setting aside specific time for training. Think about how easy it can be to "forget" to mow the lawn. You come home from work, make dinner, clean up the dishes, make a phone call, and the next thing you know, "Oh darn, it's too late, I'll just have to mow the lawn another day." This describes how many shooters treat their training; they want to do it but it's not the highest priority, so they might get it done or might not, depending on what else comes up.

If training is a priority for you, then set aside time specifically to train and budget it into your day as your highest priority for that time. An example would be dry-fire training for twenty minutes as soon as you get home from work before you do anything else. Maybe it's the first thing you do when you wake up before you get ready for work. You might find that you are more productive, or it's easier to focus at a specific time of the day. The key is having a routine you can keep and hold yourself accountable to. Having a consistent schedule will go a long way toward improvement, but it has to be a priority to get your training time in.

## Your Shooting Budget

Budgeting your finances is just as important as budgeting your training time. It is an unfortunate fact of life for most shooters that their participation is going to be limited in some way by money. That doesn't mean you should check out on any aspirations to do really well if you are short on money. Most people who win big titles in shooting are regular dudes working blue-collar jobs who are not independently wealthy. You don't need a trust fund to be a top shooter, you just need to be smart with what you have.

The way to navigate the sport with limited funds is to make a clear plan for yourself that works for you and prioritize your spending. The easiest strategy for most people is to work with a monthly shooting budget. So, if you have $500 a month you can spend on shooting (or whatever amount you can set aside), then you make a plan for $6,000 a year. The reason that this requires some forethought and planning is that expenses tend to swell up quite a lot during the big match season, and drop to near zero during the offseason. If you budget and plan properly, then you aren't going to be surprised or stressed by travel expenses when they come up.

Let's make a sample budget for our $6,000 a year shooter. Let's say they shoot Carry Optics with a Glock and plan to go to USPSA Nationals. Let's also say they want to try out some new optic and also get a new "match" gun for the year.

Right from the jump, this shooter is investing $600 for an optic and maybe a $700 gun. He plans to go to Nationals, so we can very conservatively budget $1,500 for that. There will be a plane ticket, the match fee, and lodging. We want to make sure there is some reserve cash in the hopper for any unexpected stuff as well.

With the "big ticket" items out of the way, we can look at smaller stuff. Let's say our guy is going to do three or four Section or Area matches that are within a comfortable drive for him . . . say eight hours in the car max. This can be scheduled so the matches are shot in one day, and there is only one night (the night before shooting) spent in a hotel. After the match fee, fuel, meals, etc., I would expect to spend $350–400 per match.

Adding all that stuff up, we get a total of $4,400 in expenses so far. That leaves $1,600 to feed the reloading press, pay range membership, and pay club match fees for the year. That amount of money would give maybe 10–15k rounds of ammo for training and matches. So long as our example shooter is buying and loading ammo early in the year and saving up for the travel later on in the year, they aren't going to run into a problem.

The main problem that I see when it comes to people's budgets being wrecked stems from buying guns or adding matches to the schedule they can't afford. Both of these events are usually precipitated by some sort of peer pressure. When you are on a tight budget, you need the discipline not to buy the latest gun. You need the discipline to "sit out" of a match that isn't in the budget for you. It strains relationships at home quite a bit when you decide you are spending an extra thousand dollars to fly to an Area Match at the last minute or whatever other sorts of "emergency" you create for yourself.

Have a plan and be disciplined. You can do just fine in this sport without a lot of money.

## Budgeting Mental Resources

No matter what level of participation you decide on, it is important to allocate the appropriate amount of mental "resources" to your training. It may seem odd to see "mental energy" as something finite, but it definitely is limited. Your productivity in training depends on what your goals are—correspondingly, the amount of mental capacity and emotional "toll" you are willing to take will change as your goals change.

If you are a casual shooter looking to go out to your range when you have time for some training, it is still important that you are having fun and getting something out of it. If you find that you are getting frustrated at not being able to do something, it might not be worth expending the mental resources in being frustrated and continuing with whatever isn't working for you that day. Do something else or call it a day and revisit it next time.

If you are more serious in your participation, it's probably worth it to be a little frustrated and use your mental resources to analyze the situation and figure out what is going on. You might be able to find a solution and work through that training bump. You will absolutely benefit from this, although it will come at a cost.

Ultimately, the risk of too much mental resource expenditure is burnout. This is something that will likely happen to you at some point. When it does, it might be worth taking a week off and evaluating what changes need to occur in your training plan. Properly planning and anticipating times in your training where increased mental resource expenditure might be needed is key in pushing back potential burnout. It also really helps to keep your eye on the prize of what you're really trying to accomplish long-term for the season or even for your shooting career. Burnout should be a temporary bump in the road that you can overcome by resetting your priorities and keeping your focus.

## Develop a Training Partner or Two

Having a training partner is useful in a lot of ways. A common concern about a training partner is the ability of that person. Skill level is not as important as dedication level when selecting a training buddy, but training with someone better than you can help you considerably. Training with someone weaker than you will still be helpful if they have the right approach to training. The worst situation for a training partner would be bringing someone to the range who will be a distraction for you. You want to have a training partner with similar goals to you, and one who is motivated to get better just like you are.

As previously stated, it's helpful to train with someone better than you when you can. There have been many times when a person improves from training with someone at a higher skill level. They might be able to help you locate incorrect techniques and get them corrected. You can still get a lot from training with someone who isn't at your skill level as long as they are motivated and paying attention. For example, you could tell your partner what you are working on and ask them to watch for a specific thing. An example is saying, "I am working on staying low and setting up wide when I come into a position." Regardless of skill level, your training partner can pay attention to just that part and give you real-time feedback about what they are seeing.

A significant benefit to having a training partner is having another set of eyes on your shooting. They might pick out things you don't see or have ideas for things you should try in training. I've seen a lot of benefit from taking turns setting up drills. The other person might set up situations you would have never thought of or practiced. It's also great for keeping you focused and accountable. The fact that you know someone is watching you shoot adds pressure. You don't want to make a mistake or look dumb when your friend is watching you. People are always watching you at matches, so this added pressure is realistic for the actual events you are training for.

Travel to matches and squad with your training partner if you have the opportunity. You will have someone familiar with you who knows your shooting and will have a good idea of what you can and can't do. Even though shooting is an individual sport, you can work as a "team" for coaching each other and planning stages. Most people who travel to major matches at least have an informal network of match and training buddies. It is a good system and one that you should explore.

# CHAPTER 35
# STUDYING SHOOTING

Over the course of a competitive shooting career, you will need to spend time studying in order to learn new ways to improve. There are lots of options for books, training videos, podcasts, training methods, classes, and so on for you to consider. A truly master level shooter is a perpetual student. A master is someone who never stops looking to take new things on board in order to improve, searching hours of content in search of any tip, thought, technique, or mindset that might help them advance to the next level.

The quest for excellence never ends. This section should help you parse through information with less effort, and know what is important and what you should disregard.

### Search for Actionable Items

As you go through new information, what you are looking for is something you can put into action. You may not be able to put it into action today, but you at least want to put it into action in the near future. This is an important thing to understand because it allows you to focus on things you can actually DO.

Take this example: You learn that a top shooter recommends firing 100k rounds per year of live ammunition. Due to any of a dozen reasons, that isn't in the cards for you. The recommendation for 100k rounds a year is just noise. There isn't anything you can do with that idea.

Let's say you discover a drill that you can do in dry fire, and the drill perfectly replicates and addresses some deficiency that you have in your shooting. That would be an actionable item and something that you should be very interested in implementing in your training. You are now able to train in a new way or with a new paradigm. This drill is something you want to focus on, and you have the resources to do it.

Unfortunately, so much of people's research time is spent collecting factoids about split times, reloading data, or equipment. The impulse from us (the authors) is to tell the readers to ignore irrelevant data and just focus on the important things. This begs the question, "How do I know what is important and what isn't?" Fair question.

Generally speaking, equipment and physical conditioning information is the lowest priority information to worry about. Your current equipment is probably fine provided it is appropriate for the division, and working properly. Physical conditioning takes a large amount of time and effort for a comparably small result. The most valuable information is training methods and techniques. You want to be paying the most attention to the items that allow you to improve your shooting skills, which will give you a positive outcome on all the stages you shoot.

You should be careful to try to keep preconceived notions about shooting out of your mind when you are trying to learn new things. So many shooters think they know something, but in the end, they don't quite have a perfect understanding of the concept. The fact they think they know it all prevents them from being open to learning more. This phenomenon is a problem in all areas of life, and it is going to hold you back in sport shooting just like anything else. Keeping an open mind about what you don't know is key to being able to learn and improve.

### Don't Be Afraid to Shake Things Up

After you have been training for a while, you are going to hit a plateau. This is normal and happens to everyone. It is often the case that someone will come into USPSA and get to B class very quickly with just a little training effort. At that point, the individual hits a plateau. Improvement comes slowly and with seemingly much effort.

What is needed at this point is a shakeup. New ideas and training methods need to be implemented. There needs to be specific effort applied over a period of time.

If this hypothetical shooter had been spending his time doing dry-fire on draws and reloads and then did bill drills at the range to work on shooting speed and that got him to B class, that's great. The key is, it will take something new to get him out of B class.

Even the guys at the top levels of the sport are constantly changing training and technique. This is a necessity if they want to move to a higher level for the next season. What won a National Championship five years ago, may not get it done today. That's why the top-level guys shake things up every year as they continue to improve.

### Don't Focus on Outliers

It is very common for shooters to focus on exceptions to the rule. Everyone is interested in the training techniques of the best shooters, and that is normal and natural. The important thing to remember is that by definition, champion shooters are exceptions in one way or another.

This is an important point to make because top shooters are always giving interviews and tips that the shooting community will listen to and try to glean useful information from. There is nothing wrong with that. The problem can arise when some small nugget of information is given as an answer to a question, and listeners take that and run with it without understanding the larger context of what is happening. An example is, "I always train in X way when I go to the range." Remember, they are describing a specific point in time during their training, not everything it took to get them to where they are today.

Another example would be a top shooter who comments that they only practice on half scale targets for added difficulty. That shooter may very well be doing that currently at that time in their training, but it is certainly not how they got to the level they are currently at. For most shooters that would be a terrible and ineffective way to train, since you should balance training between easy and difficult shots.

This phenomenon is especially true when the top shooter makes statements or gives advice that contradict conventional wisdom. Always keep in mind that it is difficult to get the full context or understanding of what is going on just based on small snippets of information like that.

You should focus on training ideas and concepts that work well for the majority of people and use that as your baseline for what you are doing.

## Don't Look for Magic

It should go without saying that you aren't going to find magical solutions or quick fixes for anything. Once you get into training and improvement, you will hit a plateau and improvement will come slower. That is just how it works. There are no easy paths to success. Training is a long-term commitment to improve a little bit at a time.

Understanding there is no magic to be found will help with avoiding disappointment and burnout. An example would be going to a class and firing one thousand rounds per day or taking a week off of work to train hard every day. You will see improvement, learn, and have new ideas, but you won't be a brand new shooter. Unfortunately, it just doesn't work that way.

## Books/Training Materials

The general rule with books is if you find one thing that is actionable and you can implement into your shooting, then your time was well spent reading that book. This means you will be reading plenty of stuff that you may already know or may not be able to implement right then. That isn't a problem, that is just the nature of the beast.

The general trend with shooting books is that far more copies of a book are sold than are ever actually read. Also, far more are read than the content is ever actually implemented. Usually, the problem with books is people don't actually do the work. They just read the material and don't actually implement it into their training. The intellectual knowledge of how to do something isn't really the goal here. Proficiency at doing the thing is what you want to achieve. The book can be the catalyst for learning how to train in a new way or with new techniques or a new focus, but you have to actually implement those ideas for them to actually help.

## Training Classes

Taking classes from competent instructors is a great way to learn. Many big-name instructors travel around putting on classes. It is common for traveling instructors to visit areas with large populations of competitive shooters. You should be able to find a reputable class like this at least once a year in most areas. You may also have local training opportunities in your area with competent instructors who can help you improve. Instructors who focus on competition shooting are obviously the most relevant for what you are probably trying to achieve.

The real benefit of classes is that they are live, in person, and involve feedback from someone competent to provide it. Most people train on their own and don't always understand what they are doing. Classes will involve training exercises that you can take and replicate on your own. A competent instructor will also demonstrate various shooting techniques. Things look different live and in person than they do on video.

To get the most out of a class, make sure you ask questions if you have them. Ask for clarity and direction on any techniques you aren't sure how to execute or aren't sure you are doing correctly. Ask the instructor what the big items are they think you should be working on.

The real pitfall with classes is the idea that they are going to "fix" you and make you instantly better. Classes, at best, show you how to fix yourself. You aren't going to make big improvements in technical skill in just a couple days of working with an instructor. Your goal should be to pick up a few things you want to implement in your training and work those into your training plan going forward.

## Online Forums

Message boards have been in existence for a few decades. They have some excellent uses as well as some pitfalls. Shooting forums are unexceptional when compared to other types of forums. The positive points and negative points are exactly what you would expect.

Forums tend to be excellent resources when asking specific technical questions. If you need to know how to fix something broken on your gun or reloading press, then posing the question on a forum usually works well. You are likely to get some very good information when it comes to specific technical questions. These sorts of questions are also easily searchable so you will be able to find past discussions of the same issue.

Forums fall down when it comes to getting specific answers or information for more complicated problems. It isn't so much that you can't find good information on forums. The main problem is recognizing helpful information and sorting it from unhelpful information or noise. This is essentially impossible if you don't already know the answers because the people giving the answers aren't usually vetted.

Forums tend to have extraneous chatter and interpersonal conflict as often as they have useful information. Many shooters use forums for entertainment as much as learning these days.

## Online Coaching

Online coaching is something that is relatively new to shooting sports but has been around for a few years in other sports. Digital communication has gotten accessible to the point that it is easy to quickly upload footage of yourself shooting or training. Video is generally taken with just a phone camera and then put online. The coach can then review this footage and provide feedback. Coaches can prepare training plans and interact with students over a wide geographical area. The most obvious example is Practical Shooting Training Group. This service functions just as described.

In the coming years there is no doubt that more training services will come online for shooting sports and will incorporate even more technology. Being able to use a virtual reality setup to "visit" someone in a virtual three-dimensional space and observe training is just around the corner.

Overall, using all of the tools at your disposal to assess your shooting ability and direct your training plan in the right direction to continue your development should be the goal. If you learn better from books or classes or whatever, the important thing is that you are constantly in a state of trying to improve.

# PART 10
# THE PROCESS

# CHAPTER 36

# DEVELOPING YOUR OWN PROCESSES

Throughout this book you have gained information on all of the non-shooting parts of competing in practical pistol shooting. It is more than just shooting at targets. You have learned about all of the mental aspects of shooting, as well as how to apply it to your own competition shooting. The intended audience for this book is anyone who is currently participating in, or interested in participating in competition shooting, from novice shooters to serious shooters. We have included information for shooters at all levels. If you are a more serious shooter, this book is probably more beneficial and will have more takeaways but will still provide valuable information for those just starting out or doing it for fun.

There are varying degrees of requirements and usefulness discussed in this book. From visualization to preparation and competition techniques, each shooter can take something different away from the book. Some of the things we discussed are low commitment for a shooter, but can offer a higher payoff. An example of this is walking stages and coming up with a stage plan. Less serious shooters will be ok with a hiccup now and again without it ruining their fun. More serious shooters will trade cash to reduce the probability of equipment issues in matches, often running thousands of rounds of ammunition through equipment to prevent malfunctions.

The challenge at this point is to start thinking about what you should be taking away from this material. You want to make sure that your effort is properly directed into the areas that are going to provide a big output level relative to the input. Different people with different participation levels should key in on different items.

The gut reaction that many people have is to reject this sort of thinking. They will argue they should learn everything and implement everything they have read. This is an understandable way of thinking for a Type A competitor. Being understandable doesn't make it wise though. You will need to focus on key things to take away and incorporate into your own shooting, based upon where you currently are and where you want to go.

### The Authors

The two authors of this book make for an interesting case study. Joel Park is a good shooter and is very involved in USPSA, but his situation might be considered a bit more "normal" to most readers. Joel shoots all the time as a hobby and really enjoys competing. Joel is a USPSA Grand Master and has won awards at the local and regional level. He has gone about as far as a serious but casual (meaning non-professional) can go in the sport. Joel trains regularly and devotes a lot of his free time to USPSA, both as a competitor and as an instructor. The vacation time he accrues at work is generally used to attend shooting events. To get appreciably better would require a major life circumstance change.

Ben Stoeger is wrapped up in shooting as a business, hobby, and lifestyle. Ben has devoted a significant amount of money on shooting and travel for shooting. Shooting is a career for him, and this includes teaching classes, shooting competitively, and frequently training for shooting. Ben is a seasoned competitor and international traveler. In a normal year he will visit ten countries for some sort of shooting-related event.

The important point for the reader is that each case is different. It shouldn't surprise the reader to learn that a good shooter has a different life and approach from someone who is participating at a professional level.

To help you, the reader, better understand how to apply the preceding information to YOUR actual shooting and training program, the authors have written out their own processes for competing at a match. Each one is informed by experience, participation level, and goals. Each author applies the theoretical knowledge to their own practical situation a little bit differently. By taking a look at both processes for competition, hopefully the reader can glean a little bit of insight into their own shooting and competition habits and find something to relate to.

# CHAPTER 37
# BEN'S PROCESS

**Planning My Season**

The centerpiece of my shooting season is USPSA Nationals. That is the big event of the year in the United States and the most prestigious title that you can win in USPSA. This is a "can't miss" event for people that are super serious about practical shooting inside of the United States. Once the dates for this event are known, then I can begin planning my season. It is difficult to make firm plans before.

The main idea for my seasonal plan is to show up to Nationals when I am at the peak of my ability for the year. This is a more complicated idea than it may sound like at first glance. I want to be at peak motivation and peak competitive experience, I want my gear properly tested, and I want to be in good physical condition. I will discuss each of these in turn.

Motivation—Showing up to Nationals hungry for shooting is a little bit more complicated than it sounds. I don't want to be strung out from weeks of travel. I don't want my hands destroyed from 20k rounds of training in the previous ten days. I need to be ready, but still fresh at the same time. This requires meticulous planning.

The ideal flow of a shooting season for me is to have cycles of heavy training and then cycles of matches. The idea is to have training time, then competition time, then have training time again to address the weak points that come up in matches. It also gives me time mentally to shift from "match" mode to "training" mode.

It makes a big psychological difference for me to have a long time (say six weeks) until a match. I feel free to experiment with new techniques or equipment or things like that. I can go deep into a training rabbit hole where I burn a week or two on a very specific idea or technique. I don't feel the pressure of a looming match where I want my shooting to be perfect but maybe a little bit more conservative all the time.

Things get tricky for me with a busy travel schedule that is match heavy for months on end. Training starts to feel like a job that I don't always have the energy to do properly. I may be at home for a day or two at a time and hit the range each day. At the same time, I am packing up for another trip and preparing my match gear. It gets tiring, and the motivation begins to fade.

If my motivation fades out a little bit because I am getting tired, it is generally mid-season or toward the end of the season. This is just when that extra bit of motivation is going to matter the most. I want to feel fresh and eager to train before the nationals. I don't want to feel like I need to take a break or feel like my tasks to keep my life running (take care of my place, etc.) are getting neglected too much.

This is one of those situations where it is crucial for me to know myself. I know how many weeks consecutively I can be on the road without getting burned out and wanting rest.

Of course, I can push myself through anything. I can show up at the range and train anytime. That isn't the problem. I can't manufacture the desire to train for eight hours a day. That has to be present organically. Forcing myself into long training days just means I spend a long time on the range. It doesn't mean that the training is effective.

## Competitive Experience

I want to arrive at Nationals without it being my first match of the season, obviously. Every year is a bit of a reset in competitive shooting. New competitors rise up. Some people train super hard and really make a move forward in terms of their skill. Other people lay back a little bit and kind of stay stagnant.

What I like to do is warm up with some smaller events. I like to shoot club matches to get used to shooting in front of people and to make sure I am testing myself under some sort of match pressure. I can then test myself against the field at bigger section matches or sometimes big matches in other countries. Area matches are another possibility for me, even though I haven't been to one in a couple years at this point.

I want to test myself against the field, but not too much. Again, I want to feel fresh, motivated, and hungry to shoot when I show up to nationals. I just need to feel ready for that task without being overextended at all.

## My Gear

I have a constant influx of new guns and holsters because of the volume of shooting and teaching I do. Every year a new batch of guns shows up, and I pick through them and figure out what guns will be used for what purpose. I have some guns that are training or backup guns. Then I have some princess guns that I use for matches. Over time the match guns get replaced and become training guns.

This is important because the design of the guns I use (Tanfoglio Stock 2, primarily) changes a little bit over time. Generally speaking, these changes are for the better, and I want to be using the best guns I can.

I have a whole process for testing my new guns. I feel they should shoot thousands of rounds without an issue before I can trust them. Little hiccups here and there (such as a stovepipe or light strike) are absolutely not acceptable for me. The gun should be utterly perfect. If a problem is discovered, then the testing process starts over again.

As you can imagine, this takes a little bit of time. I might be shooting a gun for a month before I am confident that it is ready to go. That means that I need to start the gear testing process early in the year to make sure that I avoid a situation where I am running up against the clock to get the gun ready for matches.

I quite simply don't like shooting guns in big matches that I haven't had proper time to test. It doesn't matter too much the brand of the gun; they all could potentially have an issue. I want to sort that stuff out early and be very confident in the gun that I use.

Ammunition is handled similarly. I might get a big lot of factory ammo that is good for matches and then spend half the lot of ammo just testing it. It gets chronographed obviously but also checked for fit with my guns and function. Not all guns like all ammo, and I really don't like leaving things to chance.

I also prepare my training ammunition well ahead of time. My training ammo is generally reloads, and during the offseason I try to load up as much as I can. It destroys my time and motivation if I need to load every night just to train the next day. I really don't like that at all, and it really lessens my desire to train, if only subconsciously. I know that every time I press the trigger, I need to load another round to replace the one I had.

### Physical Condition

I don't do a whole lot of physical conditioning (obviously). But in terms of diet and exercise, I know that I want to use the off-season time of year to accomplish fitness goals. Cutting out ten or fifteen pounds I don't need, or something like that, is best done when I am not training very heavily.

I mostly control my weight with my diet, and I know that when I am cutting weight (essentially by eating very little), my energy level is not going to be at its best. This means that during times of substantial physical activity, I will lack energy or start getting really hungry. I find that when I am shooting all day and doing physical exercise on top of it, I have a hard time restricting my food intake. It just doesn't work that well for me. This means I plan on cutting weight during the offseason.

During heavy training cycles, I am doing quite a bit more eating and working on getting stronger and faster. I know that over time my weight is going to tick up a little bit, but I kind of deem it to be worth it if I am accomplishing my shooting and fitness goals.

I try to balance these things so that I show up to nationals in pretty good physical condition, ready to do my absolute best. I don't worry a whole lot about what I am eating during the match, I just try to stay relaxed and have a good time.

### The General Flow of a Season

Because of the above factors, the way my year flows is generally an offseason then cycles of training and competition. These cycles last a few weeks at a time. It is usually three or four weeks of hard training, followed by two or three weeks of matches all over the place, and then back to training. I time things out, so when I show up to Nationals, I am feeling and shooting my best.

### Traveling

I have a pretty well-defined travel process for matches. I am a very frequent traveler; my process is streamlined pretty well, but it still may be useful for many of you.

When planning to attend a match, the key consideration for travel is whether or not I am driving to the match or flying to the match. Once I have that information figured out, it makes things quite a lot easier.

### Driving to a Match

Driving to a match is the simplest solution, and if it makes sense in terms of the time required, then it is a good option for me. Generally speaking, I don't like to drive more than twelve hours to get anywhere. When it takes longer than that to get to my destination, then I shy away from driving.

When driving, I am free to load up as much stuff as I want into my car, or someone else's car in the case of carpooling. I can take my range bag, spare guns, all the ammunition I want, etc. without a whole lot of worry. This really is the best part of traveling to matches by car. It is really quite excellent, in my opinion. The other part that I like is the complete control over stopping when you feel like it and taking detours when you feel like it.

When traveling to a match by car, my goal is to arrive at the match the day before I am supposed to shoot at the time the shooters on the range are just about finishing for the day. So, for example, if I am headed to an area match that I am scheduled to shoot on Saturday/Sunday, I want to arrive at the range about 3 or 4 p.m. on Friday. This puts me on the range when some people have finished, and some people are still shooting. In this way, the stages are just about to clear off so I can take a look at them if I like. Also, some people are still shooting, so if there is a funky prop or something, there is a good chance that I can see it in operation.

I actually think it is counterproductive to arrive super early and spend six hours on the range while people shoot. I hate standing around in the sun, not doing anything, and I really do my best to avoid showing up that early. Similarly, if I show up too late, the range is closed, or the sun has gone down, and it is pretty tough to look at the stages.

When I drive to a location, I usually do not pre-book rooms or anything like that. Most of my travel is solo, and I am not picky about where I stay. I tend to locate the range first and then just randomly select a hotel and go book a room there. This strategy presents me with minimal hassle for the most part, and because I don't like to plan things out ahead (because that locks me into particular locations and schedule), it keeps me flexible as to where and with whom I am hanging out.

After a match, I usually start for home immediately. So, if the match finishes at 5:00 p.m., I start for home at 5:15 p.m. and make as much progress as I can. It is not unusual for me to drive all night in order to get home at 3 a.m. I tend to want to wake up in my own place so I can get back to work.

## Flying to a Match

Flying to a match is a bit more complicated than driving, but not as much more complicated as you might think if you have never done it.

Most domestic carriers make traveling with guns easy. I almost always fly Delta, but I have used plenty of other airlines and never had an issue. I book domestic travel usually six to twelve weeks before the date of departure. This tends to optimize ticket prices and availability. My goal when booking a plane ticket is the same as going by car. I like to arrive at the match the day before I shoot with enough time to look at the stages.

I almost always book in a rental car at my arrival airport as well, but I do that a couple of days before the flight. If I am riding with someone, then I don't need a car. In any event, I book my travel assuming it will take sixty to ninety minutes in the airport to secure my bags and car and then get headed toward the range.

The sticking point for all this with most people is having the airline handle your gun, so I will explain the process I use.

I lock my guns in a hard-sided pistol case. A purpose-built case with proper locks is what you should be using.

If the case has more than one spot that can accept a lock, then it is usually best to have a lock there. I have had an issue where if I had one lock on a case, the inspection of that case might give me a problem if the TSA person feels they can access the gun even with a lock on the case. So, if you have two spots on the case that can take a lock, it is best just to put locks everywhere they can go, so that doesn't become an issue.

I throw my locked pistol case into a regular suitcase. I try to put it near the top of the case, so it is easy to find later. Ammunition needs to be stored in a separate container from the gun. The best practice I have found is to check a second bag and put ammunition into that bag. The second bag (the one without the gun) will be subject to quite a lot less scrutiny, so you will likely not have ammunition looked at by the airline or even weighed.

Most airlines are going to restrict you to eleven pounds of ammunition per passenger, but instances of enforcing the rule are not common. Usually, the airline asks you how much ammunition you have, and if you inform them you have less than the maximum, they typically don't check. If they do check, then things start to get a little bit fuzzy. They might weigh the ammunition and the container the ammunition is in and determine that the weight together is more than the maximum, and you are put in a situation where you need to solve that issue. I have seen a couple heated arguments with airline staff over this kind of thing. A best practice is put the ammo in a second check bag and reduce the risk of there being a discussion at all.

Most airlines have a rule about the ammunition being in "factory" containers or something like that. I have seen people have ammunition refused if they put it all loose into a bag and then put the ammo bag into their checked bag. To avoid that, just put the ammo into factory ammo boxes (even if you reloaded it). I have flown with reloaded ammo in hard-sided boxes (from Dillon or MTM) without an issue.

You might also be wise to split ammunition across your bags if you are flying with a lot of it. This, again, will help avoid even having a discussion about how much you have. Generally, people are going to fly with the ammunition at the maximum allowable weight, and you don't want to even have your ammo go on a scale because the airline scale may well be different than your scale.

When I arrive at the ticket counter to check my bag, I say, "Hi, I am traveling to Orlando (or wherever) with a firearm. The firearm is unloaded and locked in a hard-sided container inside this bag." By using the same verbiage that is inside the airline's employee manual, I am signaling to the airline staff that I know and am following the rules. Combined with frequent flyer status, the airline staff at Delta get the picture right away that I do this a lot and am not going to be a problem. My travel has been relatively trouble-free since then.

When I arrive at my destination airport, I just retrieve my bags as usual and go snag my rental car.

## Flying Internationally to a Match

Flying internationally adds another layer of complexity to the domestic matches. So, I will talk about the different considerations in turn.

The first consideration is travel time. Because of the long journey at the extra layers of complexity, I budget more time for international trips. It is best to arrive at least forty-eight hours before I plan to shoot. I don't want to arrive too much before that because I am going to be on a range training. I don't want to arrive too much after that because it starts to get risky with the potential snags that can happen with international travel. So . . . forty-eight hours is a good balance point.

You can't be flying around with guns without doing the appropriate paperwork. Every country has a different process. I don't know how many countries I have taken a gun to at this point, but the number is pretty substantial . . . The best way to figure this out is to contact the match staff (if it is a big match) or the IPSC Regional Director for that country if it is a small match. I have always gotten the correct information and been able to get a gun permit for that country. It is best to start this process months ahead of time to make sure things get taken care of on time. I have had a late start a couple times going to Canada, and the firearms office was cool and took care of it, but not every country is like that. It is far better to get going early.

You should also check to see if you need a travel visa to visit the country you are headed to. Many countries have a process for a visa, and it is very infrequently complicated, but it is something you need to do ahead of time. I use visa preparation services because they speed things up and walk you through the process. They can be expensive, but I feel that it is worth it.

For international flights, I find it just about ideal to book 90–150 days ahead of time. You want to be careful when booking this ticket. There are a few rules or potential snags to consider.

1. If possible, book your ticket, so you do not have a connecting flight inside of a foreign country. So, for example, if I have a choice of flying Minneapolis to Newark, then Newark to Prague OR flying Minneapolis to Amsterdam, then Amsterdam to Prague, I am going to take the first itinerary. Connecting in a foreign country can sometimes be a problem. In the specific case of Amsterdam, you aren't allowed to transit that airport with a firearm unless you have a local permit to do so. That itinerary would have been a problem.

2. In the case of a connecting flight in a foreign country, learn the rules, and make sure it is ok. Call as many people as you have to (airline people, regulators for that country, other shooters, whatever) until you are satisfied that you are going to be ok connecting in a foreign country.

3. Know your air carrier. If you are flying a foreign airline (as in not Delta, United, or American), then you may have a strange set of rules to consider. They may require advance permission for firearms or something like that. So, you need to check the rules of the airline and again, start making calls to get permission to do the thing you want to do. I would make these calls before I even book the ticket to make sure I am not going to have a problem. There have been situations where shooters did not get advance permission from the airline to carry a gun and then ended up having a problem at the airport. Calling ahead solves these issues.

When traveling internationally, I tend to book lodging ahead of time. Most foreign nations aren't like the United States where we have hotels at every highway exit. It doesn't work like that most places, so I tend to get way ahead of things and book an Airbnb or something, so I know I have a place to stay when I get there. Sometimes you can be asked where you are staying (like a street address) at customs, so it helps to have that information ready to go.

The final significant consideration for international travel is sleep. I have gotten pretty good at managing my sleep cycles, so I am feeling fresh when I am traveling. Basically, while I am traveling, I usually put myself to sleep (using sleeping pills), so I am pretty well-rested. It isn't uncommon for me to spend thirty hours straight in cars, airplanes, and airports without having access to a bed or a shower. Putting yourself to sleep to rest and help pass the time helps a lot.

Once I arrive at the destination country, I stay up until bedtime. This means that if I have been traveling for twenty-four hours and I arrive at 10 a.m., I am going to be up for about another twelve hours. This is accomplished with caffeine and activity. I keep myself up and busy until it is actually time to sleep in that country.

Once sleep time comes, I take sleeping pills and put myself down for eight hours. I make sure I take the sleeping pills even if I feel super tired. In my experience, I can sleep for three hours and then wake up (due to my body clock) and have a hard time falling to sleep again. I just short circuit that by taking sleeping pills, so I go down for the count.

With those considerations in mind, going to a foreign country isn't really that big of a deal. It just takes a bit more planning and foresight than domestic travel.

## Walking Through the Match

While not a thing at most IPSC matches, at USPSA matches, you are allowed to walk through the stages prior to your squad getting the written stage briefing read and the specified walkthrough time. I would actually argue that you pretty much have to show up prior to the match starting to look at the stages. There may well be complex stages with hidden targets and complicated target presentations that you just can't really figure out in five minutes. Showing up early is essential!

When I am walking through stages pre-match, I just want to get a general idea of the layout of the stages and a general plan for how I want to attack them. It is important for me not to worry too much about settling on and visualizing a specific stage plan for each stage. I want to remain mentally flexible and open to different ideas for as long as possible. As soon as you start doing specific visualization, it is difficult to look at a stage differently and you start being closed off. If you see someone else have an idea about a stage that is plainly better than your idea, it may be difficult to change your visualization, and it may be difficult even to recognize their idea is better in the first place.

For this reason, I focus on understanding the stage rather than worrying too much about a plan. Where are the targets? Is there anything strange about the stage? Is there a particular way it looks like the stage is going to flow? Are there any targets it looks like I will have trouble finding when I am on the clock? etc.

Again, I want to know the stage, but I don't worry too much about knowing how I will shoot the stage. That stuff is better left until later.

In the case that I am at an IPSC match and not allowed actually to walk on the stages, then I have the same process. Without actually walking in the fault lines, I just get a sense of the geography of the stage. Where are the targets? Where do I think I can see them from, etc. Those are the things that I am paying attention to. I think about it like this, I want to formulate a list of questions about the stage that I answer when I do the actual walkthrough inside the shooting area. Can I see this target from here or just over there? Can I shoot this target while I move? These are the things I look for when I still can't walk on the stage. It makes my proper walkthrough much faster and more effective.

## The Night before the Match

I prefer to spend my night before the match with close friends, but not with too many people around. I don't really like twenty-person dinners all that much. It complicates getting seated and takes forever. Hanging out with a couple of close guys before the match is just fine for me. It is best to avoid staying up super late or drinking. You want to be fresh and ready to go in the morning.

One thing I have found helps quite a lot is to do a bit of dry training before the match. I like to do draws and reloads and that sort of thing. It is very nice to maintain a comfort level with my equipment and work my nerves out before I am even at the range. I can do visualizations of good shooting and having the proper grip on my gun. Your state of mind is so important before the match I think it helps dramatically to get yourself in the right state of mind before you shoot.

Any negative feelings you had while walking the stages should be confronted the night before the match. If you saw a 30-yard shot on a stage that you are nervous about, don't bury that nervous feeling down deep or ignore it. You can work on your state of mind the night before the match. Pull out your gun and focus on clean trigger control or whatever cue you find helpful. You can get comfortable with the coming challenge. This isn't about building technical skills; it is about preparing you to develop the skill that you already have (if that makes sense). I find that I can effectively work through any anxiety I have about any stage by working through it mentally the night before. Failure to do this can cause you to feel behind or to have to play "catch up" mentally when you walk up to that stage the next day and are reminded of the challenge you face.

**On Match Day**

On match day, I strive to wake up two or three hours before I am supposed to shoot my first stage and arrive at the range about one hour before I shoot the first stage. This is the same process, no matter if it is a club match or nationals. The timeline doesn't change a whole lot.

On match day, I tend to eat very little until I am done shooting. The idea is never to be hungry and feel like I need to eat. I also don't want to feel like I don't have any energy. This means that I bring nuts, granola bars, or fruit. I just like having a little something to munch on if I need it, but I for sure am not looking to eat full meals.

When I arrive at the range (again, one hour before hammer down), I make sure to walk all the stages and really understand the layout of everything to the best of my ability. I don't need to mentally commit to one plan over another this early. It is good just to take a look at everything and know what questions are going to come up later on. I run these ideas by the people around me if I am curious to hear some other people's thoughts, and I am mentally ok with waiting to sort of figure things out closer to shooting time.

I like to spend the last thirty minutes or so before shooting time to check my gear, put my belt on, load my magazines, and do a bit of dry fire. It is very important for me not to get distracted by other people during this time. I am fine with casual conversation, but when it is time to walk off to the safe area and do my dry fire, then I am going to go ahead and do that no matter what other people want to talk about. My main goal during this time is to feel ready to shoot a few minutes before my squad is supposed to shoot the first stage. I generally assume I will have to shoot first even though obviously that doesn't usually happen. It just helps me get ready to assume I will not have time to do so much as fill magazines before I am supposed to shoot if I don't get it done early.

### Final Decisions

Before I actually shoot a stage, I need to decide the specific plan that I am going to shoot. I am not too worried about making these decisions very early on in the process. I don't want to close myself off to real possibilities that I see; I want to be open and ready to receive new input right up until just before I shoot a stage.

Generally speaking, I would say that I favor plans that are simple in terms of not having a whole lot of target orders that require me to memorize complicated sequences. I will tend to shoot left to right or right to left instead of some order that is, in theory, a little bit faster, but more complicated to remember. I know myself, and I know I do better with simplicity.

The other thing I try to do is to mitigate risk where I can and accept it where I can't. If there is a convenient way to leave myself some extra ammo for the array of poppers, then I usually do that. If there isn't a convenient way to leave myself extra ammo, then I will just accept the risk and plan to really aim those shots. I am not going to do complicated things, generally speaking.

There is a lot more that can be said about stage breakdown, but that was all covered earlier in the stage breakdown section. The key thing for my process is that I am delaying making these decisions, and comfortable doing so.

## Visualizing the Plan

Once I have a plan in mind, I am going to start visualizing the stage. What I am trying to do is to see in my mind's eye every task I have to do and see the tasks in order, without needing to take a second and recall something.

Let me explain briefly how this works for me. A "shooting task" is anything that will require my specific attention in order to get done. I give my attention to something by looking at it, so really I think about my list of "tasks" as a list of places where I will drive my eyes while I am shooting a stage.

Tasks include:

- Shooting a target
- Moving to a new shooting position
- Reloading
- Grabbing gun/magazines off a table
- Activating a prop (with your hands or feet)

The above list isn't exhaustive, but it should give you a good idea of what is going on mentally when I am visualizing a stage. Each task is handled by directing my eyes to the task. I am memorizing particular points on each target to drive my eyes to so the gun follows. I am visualizing looking down to my gun as I reload it. I am rehearsing, looking toward a new shooting position, and pushing myself as aggressively as I can to get to that spot. A stage is just ten, twenty, or thirty of these visual cues stacked together. That's all it is.

Now, the rule for me is to be able to see my way through the stage . . . each task . . . without needing to sit and remember anything. It needs to all be right there at the front of my mind. I can't have to think about it, or I will have hesitation when I actually shoot the stage.

During this phase of my preparation, there are a couple of other very key points I pay attention to. One of them is to make sure that I have the correct aim point on each target, especially if there is a no-shoot or a bit of hardcover to deal with on that target. I want to pick the precise location on the target that will give me the optimal outcome on average. This means I want to stay away from those no-shoots without trading out too many points. The specific aim point changes depending on what division I am shooting, but really, I don't want to risk penalties (no-shoot hits/ misses) in order to go after A's that are going to be super tough to get anyway.

I also take note of where the gun is going to be pointed if there is a movement that provides a convenient opportunity to break the safe angle on a stage. In those locations, I visualize doing the movement (or the reload or whatever) in a way that is unlikely to get me DQ'd from the match.

## When I'm on Deck

When I am a couple shooters down in the list, then I start really getting ready for the stage properly. The first order of business is a quick equipment check. This doesn't have to be a big thing, I just make sure that my gun is still on me and the magazines I plan to have on me during the stage (at least one more on me than I plan to use) are loaded up and ready to go. This is also a good time to apply grip enhancer to my hands so I can effectively hold the gun. I also take a look at the lighting conditions and make sure that I am happy with the glasses I have on. If the sun came out and I need to switch away from clear lenses or vice versa, I do so at this time.

During my "on-deck" time, I make it very clear through my body language that it is my time to prepare for the stage. I separate myself from the squad and put my head down and run those visualizations. I need to see my way through the stage in the first person without needing to think about anything as I go. I "burn-in" the key aim points on the targets (for tricky partials and such) and memorize the tricky movements.

During this time, I generally try to avoid watching the people before me shoot. I don't want them to set the pace for me, and I don't want to observe someone shoot a different plan to mine to put anything in my head. My decisions about how to shoot the stage have been made at this point, and anything that introduces uncertainty into that is potentially an issue. I strive to avoid that stuff, especially when shooting time is nearing.

If anyone wants to talk to me while I am on deck, I just politely inform that person that I am up soon. Anyone that has been around for a while is going to understand that it means I need to focus on the stage right now and can address them afterward.

## Make Ready

My "make ready" process begins just as the prior shooter is finishing their stage run. As soon as they are done, I begin my final rehearsal on the stage. I am going through one last time paying careful attention to the key tasks. If I spot a part of the stage that has potential to trip me up in some way, then I will make sure I run over that a couple times as I walk the stage that final time.

I also am applying additional grip enhancer during this time if I potentially think I might need some. I am not at all stingy with that stuff come match day. I make sure I use it if I think it will be at all helpful.

As soon as I am ready, I return to the starting position for the stage. I am hoping for a state of calm in my head. If I feel anxious, generally, that isn't usually something I am going to worry about. If I am anxious about a specific part of the stage, I continue doing mental rehearsals of that section of the stage until the last possible moment. This is unusual as I almost always feel ready, relaxed, and calm at this point.

I then stand and wait for the "make ready" or "load and make ready" (depending on the region I am in). As soon as I get the verbal command, I do a "practice draw" at full speed to make sure I am in tune with where things are. At this point in the process, there is a divergence between USPSA and IPSC, so I will cover that now.

At a USPSA match, you are allowed to draw your gun and dry fire on the actual targets. I definitely take advantage of this during my make-ready procedure. I use it as a way just to get comfortable and feel confident with how my grip is and how the gun is tracking around on the targets. I will repeat a few dry draws until I get comfortable. I then load my gun and holster it.

Once I am loaded and holstered, I dry grab my gun a few times to make sure I know exactly where it is. I don't want to have my grip missed, since that can do serious damage to my score on a stage. After my final dry grab of the gun, I nod my head and exhale while I wait for the start signal.

In the case of an IPSC match where I am not allowed to dry fire before I load the gun, I just skip that part. Instead, I do a few more dry grabs of the gun while it is in the holster. The net effect is about the same in my estimation.

If the gun is not starting loaded and holstered, then I modify my process a little bit. Instead of doing dry grabs of my gun, I will do a few repetitions of the first thing I need to do. It might be opening a door or grabbing a magazine or whatever. It doesn't make much difference.

I just do the first task of the stage a few times, if possible, and use that time to settle myself into the stage. Once again, when I am done, I settle down and wait for the start beep to come.

## Shooting the Stage

When I am shooting the stage, I accept the fact that I can't really consciously do anything to improve my situation. I am trained in the sense that I have repeated each action I will do many times in training. Those actions, be it pulling the trigger or reloading the gun or really anything that you care to mention, are all ingrained into my subconscious.

I accept that what I have trained to do is what I will do on the stage, I just keep breathing and allow the stage to happen. I am in a very observational state. I see what is happening, and I have a good recall of it. I see this, then that, then that. I watch as things take place in front of me. What I don't do is try to consciously direct things or "go fast" in certain spots or "slow down" in other places. I allow myself to do as I have trained to do and trust that it will be enough. That's it.

# CHAPTER 38
# JOEL'S PROCESS

### Preparation for the Year

In my mind, everything recycles after Nationals. Taking an off-season is very important, and I use that time to relax and enjoy my friends and family. I feel it's important that I "miss" shooting by the time the off-season is over. I use that feeling of missing shooting as fuel for training when I start back up. My away time from training is a very relaxed couple of months, and I only have a few things that I need to accomplish.

### Pre-Season Equipment Check

The first thing I worry about is checking my equipment. Any gear issues I had in the prior season need to be sorted out and addressed first thing. I do not worry about a gun that needs to be cleaned, but a malfunctioning gun gets parts replaced right away. I will shoot the gun as much as needed until I am 100 percent comfortable that it is reliable and ready for matches. Any match magazines that I do not trust 100 percent get replaced and become practice magazines.

Knowing there could be part availability issues at any time, I immediately order anything I need to have before

I start the season. I replenish my stock of spare parts and order everything I need if I am planning to make a gear change. By placing the orders now, there is no concern if something is backordered. I will not put myself in the position of really needing a part that no one has in stock during the season.

## Pre-Season Reloading

I have extra income during the winter months since I do not have any shooting expenses. I stockpile that extra money and start looking for deals on reloading components. I watch for Black Friday sales, and either organize or find group buys if needed. Once I find the best deal I think I will get, I buy everything I think I will need for the year. If the deal is really good and funds allow, I may buy even more than I need for the year.

I also start reloading ammo toward the end of my off-season. My goal is to have a stockpile of ammo to begin training with as well as a reserve that I always have just in case.

## Planning My Season

Most matches start announcing their dates around the end of the year. I keep a list of all the matches I might possibly want to attend, and I sort them all by match date. Once I have all the dates, I need to decide which matches I want to attend. I categorize them as high priority matches, and matches that would be fun, but aren't necessary. High priority matches for me are Nationals, my state match, and a few other section matches that I really enjoy and look forward to every year.

My ideal schedule is one major match every three to four weeks during the season, but I make exceptions for matches I really want to go to. I take into account how long I want my season to be and how early and late in the year I want to be training. My season usually will end with Nationals, so I need to decide how early I want to be training and when the weather will be nice enough for me to train.

Travel is another consideration. Carpooling to matches saves money on gas and hotel while making the travel less boring. Having friends to travel with does play into the deciding factor of whether I go to a match or not. I do not love to fly, but not for the reason of being scared of flying. It's a lot more expensive, I might want to ship ammo, and I am always nervous my luggage will get lost on the way to the match. I always breathe a sigh of relief when my luggage shows up on the baggage claim.

I start filling in my calendar with the matches I absolutely want to go to, then I see what spaces I have open. I plan on a two-week break somewhere around the middle of the season. It's an optional break, and I build it in just in case I'm tired or need to step away. Looking at the remainder of my calendar will then show a few empty spaces, and I will pick from the medium priority matches to fill in my calendar.

Once I have the matches picked for my season, I wait until registration opens, and I sign up for every match I can during January and February. This will be the last shooting expense I have until I travel to my first major match for the year.

Once I register, I coordinate with my friends to make sure we can all squad together. Spending time with my friends is a priority, and it makes the match so much more fun when I can spend the weekend with my friends.

## Outlook on My Personal Shooting

I am highly motivated to get better, and I absolutely love training. I enjoy live-fire training sessions more than I enjoy going to matches. I am also strange in the fact that I really enjoy dry fire. I am very motivated by being the best I can possibly be, and I get a lot of enjoyment from helping friends and teaching classes.

I put my heart into shooting, and I do not have any delusions of being a National Champion. I do train hard and want to be a mercenary at the club and state level. I hope to win an Area match someday and think it might be possible. I will be perfectly ok if it doesn't happen, though. In all honesty, I would say my greatest enjoyment from shooting is the process of training, getting better, training other people, and the time I get to spend with my friends. Being completely honest with myself helps me keep things in perspective. I spend a lot of time, money, and energy on training. I understand that I would have to make a major change to win a Nationals, and that is not a commitment I'm willing to make at this point.

## Training Schedule

I work a regular 8:00–5:00 job, and I organize the majority of my schedule outside of work around shooting. My family and friends always come first, but outside of that, I have lots of time I set aside for training.

I usually dry fire daily, including the weekends. It's too easy to get sidetracked and run out of time for training.

I set aside time so my training takes priority, and it's the first thing I do as soon as I get home from work. A typical dry-fire session is fifteen to sixty minutes. I usually have a specific focus or skill in mind, and I prefer "variable setup" drills. Variable setup drills mean I do not set up the exact same drills over and over. Instead, I set up the targets differently in each drill as I focus on improving a specific skill. I might change the drill after five minutes, or it might be fifteen minutes. It all depends on how I am feeling, and how things are going. I feel like I am good at assessing my practice sessions. I know myself well enough to know when things are highly productive, and when I am no longer benefiting from practice that day.

I switch gears toward a "putting it all together" type of training if I'm within a few days of a major match. The goal is to make myself comfortable, prove to myself that I am ready, and I can put it all together in a match. An example would be to shoot some targets, move to another position as I reload, then shoot more targets. The benefit for me is building confidence right before a match more than building skill.

My live fire training is usually every Saturday and Sunday unless there is a match that day. I often add a practice on a weekday or two depending on my schedule that week, and proximity to a major match. I will usually increase the training frequency the week of a major match.

I always have a plan in mind before I get to the range. Half of my practice sessions are stand and shoot fundamentals practice, with the other half being scenarios or drills with movement. If I am ever in a crunch for time, I will work on stand and shoot drills because of the fast cleanup and setup.

In the past, I would shoot 500–600 rounds per practice, and now that number is probably closer to 400 rounds with a higher training frequency. Meaning, I shoot roughly the same number of rounds yearly, but spread out over more trips to the range. I've found I learn more and see an increase in skill by training with higher frequency. I realized I wasn't learning as much at the end of higher round count training sessions, and it started to feel like "going through the motions." This theory is proven by how effective daily twenty-minute dry fire is compared to a two-hour block of dry fire once a week.

My usual training method is shooting three to four runs on a drill then scoring in aggregate as I'm looking for trends and consistency. My live training mirrors my dry training that I push to improve my skills for the majority of the season, then I switch to "match mode" or "putting everything together" the week before a major match. The goal is to build my comfort level and prove to myself that I can put all the skills together without pushing too hard.

### Driving to a Match
Driving to the match is definitely my preference if it's within twelve hours. I appreciate the comfort of being able to bring more than I need, and I do not have to be at the mercy of anyone delivering my luggage. I bring a cooler already filled with drinks, range snacks, jacket, rain jacket, more ammo than I'll need, etc. I want for absolutely nothing at matches and want the feeling of always being prepared. I'll rarely need to locate a store before the match for something I need or forgot. I prefer to carpool, and traveling with my friends makes traveling more enjoyable.

If the match is going to be on a hot day, I start hydrating the day beforehand. I try not to annoy my passengers with making too many restroom breaks, but I make sure to drink fluids all day. I have learned the lesson about not hydrating the hard way, and it makes for a miserable day.

## Flying to a Match

As I mentioned, I do not love flying. The travel itself is fine, but my luggage showing up always makes me nervous. I prefer to ship ammo ahead of time to the match if they have accommodations to do so. I typically ship around 200 rounds more than the required round count for the match. I ship it the week before the match, so I have delivery confirmation before I leave my house. I realize some of my processes might seem like overkill, but I set myself up to have absolutely nothing to worry about other than the actual match and my shooting performance.

For luggage, I have two bags; a carry-on bag with all my clothes and hygiene items, and a second bag that I check. The checked bag has a Pelican hard-sided case with my guns and mags locked inside, as well as any other items I need to bring that can't be put in a carry-on due to TSA rules, such as tools. I also bring a backpack of some kind that I plan to use for my range bag filled with the things I absolutely need, such as mag brush, extra fiber rods, and my holster rig.

Regardless of the travel method, when I arrive in the city, my priority is to get to the range. The only exception is if they have shooters shooting the day I plan to walk the stages, I really don't want to arrive until they are about finished. If I have a friend shooting that day, I will message them for intel and try to arrive around the time everyone is done shooting so I can walk on the stages.

### Walking Stages

When I get to the range, I change into my range shoes, apply sunscreen immediately, and bring drinks with me as I continue to hydrate myself. I check in at the match first thing, then locate my match ammo (if applicable).

My goal is to see absolutely everything I need to see, but not stay on the range any longer than I need to. This is especially true on hot summer days. I also pay attention to how the range is arranged, how the stages are numbered. I check if there will be water available for competitors at the match. That info will affect my grocery store trip later that night, so I know how many drinks I need to bring.

I get a copy of the matchbook and walk all the stages. I decide on stage plans for the most part unless there is an activator, disappearing target, or something else that I am unsure of. I wouldn't say I have the plans absolutely 100 percent burned into my brain, but I have a pretty good idea of what I want to do. If I see a better stage plan on match day, I am still able to change my mind if needed. My theory on this is, the execution of the plan is more important than the plan itself the majority of the time. As a general rule, I look for the simplest plan that will be the easiest to memorize. There are stages that require a complicated plan to have a good score, and that is a different situation. I feel more comfortable having a majority of the stages planned. It helps me sleep easier knowing all the research is done, and all I need to do on match day is worry about shooting.

For memory stages, I will take all the time I need so I can feel comfortable. I make sure I know where every target is, make sure I am only counting each target once, and will decide on a plan 100 percent. Once I have my plan, I have a friend I trust check to make sure I am not missing anything. On match day, I will not be interested in what anyone else is doing on those stages. I will be happy to share and explain my plan, but I will not change my plan unless there is something really wrong or missing.

## The Night Before a Match

After leaving the range, I'll head to the hotel to check-in. I make hotel reservations beforehand, and I am a creature of habit. I will usually stay at the same hotel every year if it's close to the range, and I had a good experience previously.

If I flew, I will make a grocery store trip before the night is over. I buy more food and drinks than I think I will need. I like being the guy with extra snacks to share, and I do not want to be in the position that I need to ask someone else for something I'm missing.

Group dinners are fun the night before the match, and something I look forward to. I prefer a smaller group for the convenience of reservations and getting a table. My dinner preference is something with protein, usually a steak or burger. I might order soda with dinner, but I also order a water if it's going to be hot the next day. The rest of my night will be hanging out with friends as I am mindful of continuing to drink fluids.

I rarely dry fire the night before the match. I will not make myself any more comfortable or prepared than I already am, and I don't want my hands to be sore. I do not think or worry about shooting, I don't worry about what is going to happen the next day. I enjoy the down time I get to spend with my friends, and I go to bed whenever I get tired.

## Match Day Behavior

On the morning of the match, I set my alarm for fifteen minutes earlier than I need to wake up. I take my time showering and getting ready. I do not want to feel rushed. I don't eat a heavy breakfast, and I usually have a protein bar. I get to the match thirty to forty-five minutes before I need to report to my first stage. That gives me plenty of time to put on my gear, load my magazines, and walk the first few stages again.

I dry fire in the safe area a bit to make sure my holster position is correct when I put my belt on. Doing some fast draws helps me feel more comfortable and assures me that my gear is positioned exactly how I need it to be. I also press the trigger fast while making sure I am not moving the sights, and do some presses in double action. My dry fire might be two minutes, and it might be five. I stop when I feel comfortable.

I am always a little nervous on my first stage, and I pay extra attention to the things that could go wrong for me based on previous experiences. Examples for me would be:

- making sure I do not shift my vision from the last target in an array until I am done shooting it
- extra visualization aiming at the A boxes on the targets and not just squirting bullets at them
- letting my sights settle as much as they need to be on a far target

- staying in control and knowing I am fast enough
- knowing I need to stick to my plan regardless of how fast or accurate someone else is

I usually feel a lot more relaxed after the first stage. My goal is to execute my plan and shoot to my ability regardless of what others do. I am not skilled at tracking the results throughout the match. If I'm squadded with my closest competition, I will usually have an idea of where I'm at, but I will not know for sure. I do not trust my ability of tracking scores enough to do anything with the data. Someone with those skills might tell me the score, I might be curious and check the results electronically, or I might not know until the match is over.

Regardless of what I learn, I make a conscious effort of not throttling up or down based on the results. If I am in the lead, I do not throttle down because I might let off the accelerator too much and find myself in second place. If I'm in second place, I will continue to execute my plan regardless of what happens. I have tried pushing to gain ground enough times to know it rarely works, and usually has a bad outcome. I am also aware that pressure is probably affecting the other competitors, and they could crash under the pressure the same as me. Anything can happen on the last few stages of a match as pressure builds and people get more tired. My goal is to just shoot my match and try not to be affected by anyone else around me.

If it's a match that needs to have a break for lunch, I try to stay focused on the match. I will rarely have the match lunch and prefer to stay on the range unless it's extremely hot, cold, or raining. For most matches, I will set up in the shade on the stage I need to be at following lunch. I leave my belt on and probably will leave my gun in the holster. I might take off my magazines and put them in my range bag, but otherwise I am ready for the next stage.

I would describe my state as not "checked out," but definitely not keyed up either. I enjoy chatting with my friends, but I remember the reason I am there. I continue to hydrate and snack on the food I brought with me as I rest in the shade. If I am feeling a little tired, I will have an energy drink with lunch. I do not want to drag out lunch and will be ready to continue the match whenever the Range Officers are on the stage and ready for us. By keeping some shooting focus at lunch, I feel less "first stage jitters" when we start back up for the afternoon.

## When I'm on Deck

I will usually continue to reset the stage until I'm "on deck." I don't need to overthink the stage to death. I just need to know where the targets are so I can shoot them. I apply grip enhancer very specifically if needed. The way I check if my hands are dry enough is that I make a fist with my firing hand and place my support hand around it. I squeeze my support hand as hard as I will when I'm shooting and see if the fingers of my support hand slide on my fist. I am ready if my hands stay together, and I need to apply grip enhancer if my hands don't stay together or slip. I only apply grip enhancer to my support hand and the back side of my firing hand. I do not want the palm of my firing hand completely dry. I need to be able to shift the gun in my hand to hit the magazine release, and I want to be able to fix a mis-positioned grip or draw if I end up with one.

I visualize the stage over and over while I'm waiting to walk the stage. I should be able to visualize the stage from beginning to end in first person. If there is anything I am unclear on, I will make sure to get the answers I need as soon as I can walk on the stage.

After the "unload and show clear" range command for the prior shooter, I walk the stage again. I pay extra attention to anything I was unsure about while I was visualizing. I walk through the stage exactly how I plan to shoot it. I will continue to do that until the last resetters are heading up range, and I'll walk back with them. If there is a slowdown or they aren't ready for me, I will stay on the stage and not assume the ready position until they are wrapping up. My goal is to not have the match staff waiting on me, or need to be "called" to the line. I want to be ready when they are waiting for me, but I also do not want to be standing in the start position with nothing to do other than getting nervous.

**Make Ready**

If I am ever unclear if I have been told to make ready, I will ask the Range Officer directly, "Did you say make ready?" After I have been given the command, I draw the gun a few times, get a few trigger presses, load the gun, chamber check, de-cock, and holster. I might hear talking or laughing behind me. I assume they are too busy talking to each other and have no interest in my shooting. I leave my hand on my gun as it's in the holster and I do not remove it until I'm ready. When I'm ready, I release my hand from the gun and move it to the starting position, give a slight nod, and remain still.

As I wait for the buzzer, I do not have any thought. It's all programmed, and I'm just going to do the exact same thing I've been visualizing. I do not make any speed adjustments as I'm shooting. I have learned not to trust my perception of time as I shoot. I can't trust any of the feelings I have during a stage. I just shoot the stage the way I have programmed.

## Shooting Club Matches

My local club matches are important matches for me. They are six stages to seven stages, and they are held monthly. I place a lot of importance on them since it is the best way I have to check myself outside of major matches.

I approach club level matches with the same level of preparation as Nationals. I won't have access to stage diagrams ahead of time, but I want to treat the match with the same level of professionalism. I get to a local match an hour early to walk stages. If I'm setting up a stage, I get there an hour and a half early. Regardless of who shows up, I want to do my absolute best. There might be someone there who can challenge me, and there might not be. In either case, I want to perform to my ability and train myself to compete the way I want to at Nationals.

## Stage Design

I enjoy setting up stages and have learned a lot by doing it. I have my stage diagram drawn up before I get to the range, and the written stage briefing already typed out. I am lucky to have friends that are willing to help me set up my stage. By having my diagram ready, there is always clear direction about what supplies are needed, and roughly where everything needs to go. I want to maximize the amount of help I get with setup and be efficient.

The first thing I do is get all the props on the range and set them up in a general idea of where I think they will need to be. As my friends help me set up, they might not place everything exactly how I had it in mind. I do not have any emotional attachment to stage design, and I do it to be helpful at my club. I'll make some changes that I think need to happen, but all I care about is an interesting and fun stage.

Once everything is roughly in place, I set some fault lines on the ground and then walk through the stage through the eyes of a "shooter." I look for places I would exploit the stage, or things that I think limit your options. Anything unsafe or possible ways to "game" the stage are changed right away. After I have fixed everything I see, I ask a friend or two to check the stage. I usually pick a few of the veteran shooters that have more experience. After I get the go ahead from them, we nail down all the target stands and walls, and I'm ready to walk the rest of the stages.

## Walking Stages

The procedure of walking stages is no different than an Area match or Nationals. I walk them with my friends, we compare ideas, and come up with the best plans we can. Squads can get mixed, moved, or shuffled, so I decide on my stage plans before the match starts. I could be up first on the first stage, and I get a lot of comfort by feeling prepared. I am probably 80 percent committed to my plan before the match starts, if I had to put a number on it. I can change my plan if I need to, but unless I see something big, I am not going to change anything.

After I have my stage plans, I put on my belt and head to the safe area. I do some dry fire in the safe area the same as I would at a major match. After I feel comfortable, I go back and load my magazines and then chat with my friends until the match briefing starts.

## Match Results

Club matches are more relaxed because everyone knows each other. I enjoy spending time with my friends, but I want my performance to be the same it would be at any major match. I do not joke around with anyone who is getting ready to shoot, and I stop interacting with people when I'm within a few shooters. The rest of the time I enjoy socializing, and I'm mindful of where others are in the shooting order so I can be respectful.

Regardless of win or lose, I pay attention to the results. On a six-stage local match, I could have a bad stage and still win. I have to put that into perspective of how it would affect the scores at an area or section match. Mistakes at matches sting a lot and get addressed in training.

## Small Local USPSA Matches and Miscellaneous Other Matches

Most cities have informal small weekly matches. They are usually on a weeknight after work, and could be anything from a two-stage indoor match, small outdoor match at night under floodlights, bowling pin match, bullseye match, etc. Most people attend these matches after work as a social gathering with their friends. There isn't usually very much tension between competitors and the entire event feels relaxed and fun.

I will be blunt: Absolutely anything can happen at this type of match, and I wouldn't read much into the results. Now that we have that baseline, let me explain.

In a six-stage match, you could have a miss and no-shoot on a stage, and the average of your other five stages bring up your score enough that you still do well. The larger match rewards consistency. In a two-stage match, one miss could cause a 10–20 percent difference in your score. That is a huge margin for only one error. To compare, a miss in a six-stage club match might only affect the scores 2–5 percent, depending on the hit factors and total points available.

You can still test your shooting ability and how you handle pressure at these small matches. However, be careful about thinking you are improving or getting worse from such a small sampling of stages. The main goal for most people is having a fun event with friends. Often at these matches, it's a great chance for me to focus on other people's performance as well, particularly any local competitors who I have had the pleasure of training. It gives me the chance to see them in action at a match, and I'll often take note of things I see that I want to bring up with them at a future training class.

I attend these smaller local matches and I enjoy them. My goal fairly often is to just enjoy spending time with my friends more than measuring my own progress. Don't get me wrong, I am there to win and do my best, but I will not lose sleep if someone beats me. I would say my head is "in the game"—it's not like I'm just going to sling lead and not care, I WANT to win—but I don't give those matches a second thought after they're over. Head-to-head types of competitions such as bowling pin matches are exceptionally fun, and sometimes it can come down to luck in addition to skill. These experiences are also helpful for learning to deal with match pressure since there are a lot of people watching and cheering, and you're on the line directly competing with another shooter.

## Gear Maintenance

Having reliable gear is very important to me. I have three Tanfoglio Stock 2's that are as close as I can get them to being identical, and I tell them apart by the color of the grips. My match gun stays pristine, it is only used for matches, and I replace all the springs at least yearly. Any part that I suspect will be an issue gets replaced before it fails. There will always be variables that can't be controlled, but I want to do everything I possibly can to set myself up for success.

My backup match gun is also pristine. I have shot it enough to trust it 100 percent , and it stays clean and ready whenever I need it. I only use it in the event of my match or practice gun going down. It is my safety net. I am not dismissive of issues on either match gun. Issues usually happen for a reason, and I am very sensitive to the condition they are both in.

My practice gun sees all my dry fire and live fire practice. I am not particular about it, and it sees a heavy volume of use. I keep it clean enough to know it will run 100 percent in practice, but I will usually just leave the springs in it until it breaks or has reliability issues. Heavy amounts of use will teach you how dirty it can get before it has problems. By doing this, I can reliably predict when parts need to be replaced in my match guns and how often they need to be cleaned.

I broke some slide stops back when I shot CZ handguns. Whenever one broke in my practice gun I would move the slide stop from my match gun to my practice gun and place a new slide stop in my match gun. Rotating parts in that might make sense depending on the gun and type of part.

I keep "match," and "practice" magazines separate also. The theme is keeping things I will use in matches as nice as I possibly can. Once magazines get in too bad shape to be used for practice, they become dry-fire magazines that stay loaded with dummy rounds and never go to the range again.

I load my "match" ammo months before any matches. I check every round in a hundo case gauge and place my match ammo in 100-round ammo boxes. When case gauging, anything that fits just a little too snug or feels out of the ordinary automatically goes in ammo cans with the rest of my practice ammo.

The reoccurring theme is, I try to be as prepared as I possibly can be in all of my preparation. There can still be random issues, breakage, or sometimes things just happen outside your control.

# CHAPTER 39

# ARE YOU READY?

Are you ready? The next time you are at a match, you should really consider that question after you get done with a stage. How did you feel when the beep went off? How did your stage run go? I will submit to you, the reader, that if you are not truly ready to shoot a stage, you are going to know it, and you are going to feel it. Trust this feeling.

The issues discussed in this book, things about mental preparation, visualization, strategy, and so forth, are all things that should help you get ready to shoot a stage. So many people get up to shoot a stage and give the nod when the Range Officer asks, "Are you ready?" But the fact is, they aren't really ready.

Using the things discussed in this book can help you spend your time getting ready, so you can shoot at your absolute best. The key thing that you, as a shooter, should keep in mind is to pay attention to your thoughts and emotions when you are at a match. You are going to pick up on little challenges you don't feel ready for or stages you don't understand how to shoot properly. Don't bury that stuff, pay attention to it so you can fix it later. Over time, you will learn to anticipate and rectify these issues before they become a problem.

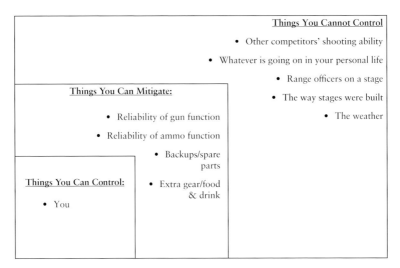

Figure 13: Earlier in this book, we made a simplified chart of what you can and cannot control, and through your reading, you should have discovered this goes a bit deeper. You can control yourself and how you react as well as mitigate things that may cause you issues along the way.

In addition to the normal things like regular dry fire and live training, there is a whole different dimension to your shooting performance. This different dimension is paying attention to your thoughts, feelings, and emotions' during a match and then adjusting your preparation, so you are in a better mental state the next time. I encourage you to get into this mode where you are always working to make yourself a stronger competitor for the next match. To win, you need to be a well-rounded competitor, in both mind and technical ability. Once you have both dimensions dialed in you are poised to maximize your performance.

# GOAL CHARTS

| MAIN GOAL | |
|---|---|
| I WANT TO: | QUANTIFY IT: |
| | |

| WHERE I AM CURRENTLY: | |
|---|---|
| MY STARTING POINT IS: | MY GOAL IS REALISTIC FROM HERE: |
| | |

| SUB-GOALS NEEDED TO REACH MAIN GOAL: | |
|---|---|
| I NEED TO: | QUANTIFY IT: |
| | |
| | |
| | |

| I WILL REEVALUATE THIS GOAL: |
|---|
| |

| MAIN GOAL | |
|---|---|
| I WANT TO: | QUANTIFY IT: |
| | |

| WHERE I AM CURRENTLY: | |
|---|---|
| MY STARTING POINT IS: | MY GOAL IS REALISTIC FROM HERE: |
| | |

| SUB-GOALS NEEDED TO REACH MAIN GOAL: | |
|---|---|
| I NEED TO: | QUANTIFY IT: |
| | |
| | |
| | |

| I WILL REEVALUATE THIS GOAL: |
|---|
| |

# ACKNOWLEDGMENTS

Many people have helped or supported the creation of this book. There are too many to name them all.

The group of proofreaders for the ideas, corrections, and additional content they suggested.

Jarel Jensen for rearranging his schedule and vacation to take proofing the book as seriously as a full-time job.

Ben: Tim Meyers hassles me about deadlines and keeps me on task. Joel Park once again contributed the majority of the brainpower. Countless others helped me in some way . . . there are too many to mention.

Joel: My parents for always being supportive and an important part of my life. Many people have influenced my shooting over the years; there are too many to name and I am very grateful.

Practical Shooting Training Group (PSTG) is an entirely online coaching platform. The site contains drills with video explanations and written diagrams, training video, and a venue to get feedback on student submitted videos.

Available online at: www.pstg.us

# OTHER TITLES WITH SKYHORSE PUBLISHING

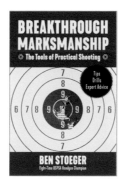

*Breakthrough Marksmanship*
Ben Stoeger
120 Pages
ISBN: 978-1-5107-7936-5
Price: 15.99

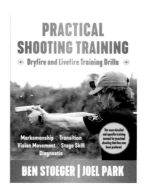

*Practical Shooting Training*
Ben Stoeger, Joel Park
336 Pages
ISBN: 978-1-5107-7934-1
Price: 29.99

*Practical Pistol*
Ben Stoeger
216 Pages
ISBN: 978-1-5107-7948-8
Price: 24.99